Studies in Curriculum Theory Series
Series Editor: William F. Pinar, University of British Columbia, Canada

In this age of multimedia information overload, scholars and students may not be able to keep up with the proliferation of different topical, trendy book series in the field of curriculum theory. It will be a relief to know that one publisher offers a balanced, solid, forward-looking series devoted to significant and enduring scholarship, as opposed to a narrow range of topics or a single approach or point of view. This series is conceived as the series busy scholars and students can trust and depend on to deliver important scholarship in the various "discourses" that comprise the increasingly complex field of curriculum theory.

The range of the series is both broad (all of curriculum theory) and limited (only important, lasting scholarship) – including but not confined to historical, philosophical, critical, multicultural, feminist, comparative, international, aesthetic, and spiritual topics and approaches. Books in this series are intended for scholars and for students at the doctoral and, in some cases, master's levels.

Curriculum Histories in Place, in Person, in Practice
The Louisiana State University Curriculum Theory Project
Edited by Petra Hendry, Molly Quinn, Roland Mitchell, Jacqueline Bach

Women Curriculum Theorists
Power, Knowledge and Subjectivity
Sandra Leaton Gray, David Scott

Love in the Post-Reconceptualist Era of Curriculum Work
Deliberations on the Meanings of Care
Jean Michel Jales Coutinho

more information about this series, please visit: https://www.routledge.
/Studies-in-Curriculum-Theory-Series/book-series/LEASCTS

Love in the Post-Reconceptualist Era of Curriculum Work

By employing the autobiographical method of *currere* and bifocalization, this book sheds light on the significance of love and the ethics of caregiving as means to transform curriculum studies into a post-reconceptualist and collective endeavor.

Advancing an understanding of curriculum as a "collective public moral enterprise," it critically asks whether we can build a world where love is not negotiated, but only proliferated. Through the creation of short and interconnected autobiographical narratives about the meanings of love, the author provides pivotal insights for curricularists who labor in conflicting and paradoxical contexts. As such, the book seeks to demonstrate how the labor of "love fortification" may be accomplished in a world of agonistic, antagonistic, and competiti becoming(s). Highlighting the role of caregiving, this book questi the role of evaluations in post-reconceptualization and provides insi for educators and policymakers on how to promote "actualization reconciliation in schools in contexts across the global-north and -

Engaging with a long scholarly tradition that ultimately s understand the meanings of love in our lives and in our work, ing the "historization" of the field of curriculum, and with a tional focus, this book will appeal to scholars and stud interests in curriculum studies and curriculum theory.

Allan Michel Jales Coutinho is a doctoral student at the l British Columbia, Canada. His scholarly work also cul academic experiences at the University of Toronto, Ha University, Green Mountain College, and the Fede Institutes of Science, Technology, and Education.

Love in the Post-Reconceptualist Era of Curriculum Work
Deliberations on the Meanings of Care

Allan Michel Jales Coutinho and
Foreword by William F. Pinar

NEW YORK AND LONDON

First published 2023
by Routledge
605 Third Avenue, New York, NY 10158

and by Routledge
4 Park Square, Milton Park, Abingdon, Oxon, OX14 4RN

Routledge is an imprint of the Taylor & Francis Group, an informa business

© 2023 Allan Michel Jales Coutinho

The right of Allan Michel Jales Coutinho to be identified as author of this work has been asserted in accordance with sections 77 and 78 of the Copyright, Designs and Patents Act 1988.

All rights reserved. No part of this book may be reprinted or reproduced or utilised in any form or by any electronic, mechanical, or other means, now known or hereafter invented, including photocopying and recording, or in any information storage or retrieval system, without permission in writing from the publishers.

Trademark notice: Product or corporate names may be trademarks or registered trademarks, and are used only for identification and explanation without intent to infringe.

Library of Congress Cataloging-in-Publication Data
Names: Jales Coutinho, Allan Michel, author. | Pinar, William F., writer of foreword.
Title: Love in the post-reconceptualist era of curriculum work : deliberations on the meanings of care / Allan Michel Jales Coutinho; foreword by William F. Pinar.
Description: New York, NY : Routledge, 2023. | Series: Studies in curriculum theory | Includes bibliographical references and index.
Identifiers: LCCN 2022057027 (print) | LCCN 2022057028 (ebook) | ISBN 9781032417615 (hardback) | ISBN 9781032418353 (paperback) | ISBN 9781003359968 (ebook)
Subjects: LCSH: Education--Curricula--Social aspects. | Love--Study and teaching. | Critical pedagogy.
Classification: LCC LB1570 .J26 2023 (print) | LCC LB1570 (ebook) | DDC 375--dc23/eng/20221230
LC record available at https://lccn.loc.gov/2022057027
LC ebook record available at https://lccn.loc.gov/2022057028

ISBN: 978-1-032-41761-5 (hbk)
ISBN: 978-1-032-41835-3 (pbk)
ISBN: 978-1-003-35996-8 (ebk)

DOI: 10.4324/9781003359968

Typeset in Times New Roman
by SPi Technologies India Pvt Ltd (Straive)

To those who have and who are still going to seek and bifocalize in the course, a calling to fortify love

Contents

Foreword ix
Acknowledgments xv

1 Introduction 1

2 Studying love through juxtapositions in curriculum 11

　2.1 The way we go about loving: understanding "love" in curriculum, within and across con(texts) 14

3 Positioning love as an ethics of care/giving in curriculum 34

　3.1 The way we go about caring: understanding convergences and divergencies 42

4 Unfolding autobiographies, fortifying love in curriculum 55

　4.1 Parental love 57
　4.2 Religious love 60
　4.3 Brotherhood love 66
　4.4 Romantic love 69
　4.5 Labor love 72
　4.6 Converging through and with care: from crises to proliferation 75

viii Contents

5 Love and justice in evaluations in societies and in schools   81

    5.1 Evaluations and generalizations 85
        5.1.1 Evaluations in the world of legal systems 89
        5.1.2 Evaluations in the world of school systems 94
    5.2 Actualization in post-reconceptualization: an autobiographical account 96

6 Conclusion: love and reconciliation   109

Index   112

Foreword

William F. Pinar

Too often love seems in short supply, sometimes even in private life. Certainly, it seems to have slipped away from the public sphere. Take, for example, the research of Charlotte Brand, Alberto Acerbi and Alex Mesoudi, research that analyzed more than 150,000 pop songs released in the United States between 1965 and 2015. During that period, the occurrence of the word "love" in the top 100 hits fell by 50 percent. Meanwhile, the incidence of such songs conveying negative emotions—specifically hate—increased sharply.[1] Other evidence of love's "decay"[2] comes not from pop culture but from journalism. David Rozado, Ruth Hughes and Jamin Halberstadt analyzed 23 million headlines published between 2000 and 2019 appearing in 47 different news outlets popular in the United States. They found that there, too, love was in short supply, as headlines had become increasingly negative, emphasizing events associated with "anger, fear, disgust and sadness."[3] During the past two decades, they found that deadlines in left-leaning media had become increasingly negative; headlines in right-wing or right-leaning publications were even worse.[4] "The negativity in the culture reflects the negativity in real life," David Brooks suggests.[5]

A recent Gallup survey of 150,000 people in 140 countries signals that the situation is even worse outside the United States.[6] Stress, sadness, angry, sorry and physical suffering all showed up at historical highs. (Gallup conducts this survey each year.) "We live in a world of widening emotional inequality," Brooks observes, as the top 20 percent of humanity reports high levels of happiness and wellbeing while the bottom 20 percent reports low levels.[7] "The emotional health of the world is shattering," Brooks concludes.[8] And it was never—to stay with Brooks' gerund—exactly intact.

What's love got to do with it?, you might ask. You can't eat love if you're hungry. Nor does it provide a roof over your head if you're homeless. If you're a solder on a front line in Ukraine, loving your enemy could get you killed. But love could—does—prompt many to share food with those without it, provide shelter to those stuck on the street, press politicians to negotiate peace. Food, shelter, and peace may be prerequisites for staying alive, but love makes being alive worthwhile. The promise of love is what Christianity communicates, as do other institutionalized (and non-institutionalized) religions.[9] Faith may affirm the power of love to those who listen to the ordained, but too many others sitting uncomfortably in church pews hear prompts for self-righteousness, sexual repression, racial superiority. Much of what plagues the planet can be traced to failures of the Church, and that institution has had – presumably – God on its side. Can curriculum achieve what catechism cannot?

Don't count on it, Jales Coutinho seems to say. In fact, due to pervasive "hierarchization and unprincipled competition," he knows, "people may be inclined to position love as make-believe." Materializing "make-believe" is, I suggest, exactly what this text achieves: Jales Coutinho makes love in front of your eyes. In part curriculum theory, in part prayer—that last term invoking the legendary James B. Macdonald's very conception of curriculum theory—Jales Coutinho theorizes how we might study and thereby materialize this omnipresent—if accented by its heart-aching absence—aspiration. This text is a labor of love, a text of admirable erudition, self-excavation, and scholarly explication, all enacted as this most remarkable scholar—as "seeker"—studies the ways curriculum studies has grappled with the ongoing crisis that is humanity. Wisely, shrewdly, he starts with himself:

> Every time I step out of my door which is my self, I am asked to meet someone's else hospitality, but it seems that I have lost my own, for I can no longer give with a full heart. I now wonder what has been left of my humanity: *will the course ever be able to gift it back to me?* At this historical juncture, I do not think so. My only option then is to try to change it by seeking and studying, by returning to genesis, to love.

As Coutinho knows, studying the words of others provides signposts for each of us journeying on a path that is uncharted, a course on which one might—with study—find one's way, might find love. While that love may be embodied in another—a loved one—studying one's educational experience of curriculum can constitute a labor of love, a course to be run on one's own if also in the company of others. No finish line—except death—no winners or losers in this running of the Course, only the fundamental fact, curriculum as a "collective public moral enterprise," a curriculum of love.

This text testifies to love as reconciliation, a secular version of Christian redemption, yes one's own but hardly only one's own, as in the absence of others love is utterly elusive, an aspiration—laudable and necessary as aspiration is—but not (yet) material reality, "both in global-north and -south contexts." Such elusive love becomes, for Jales Coutinho, in this "Post-Reconceptualist" era, tortuously tenuous, requiring "fortification." The mind may be no muscle but there are movements in the running the course that affirm fortification, specifically ongoing engagement with alterity, curriculum design construed as "juxtaposition," design encouraging "bifocality." Feet on the ground, decoding the signposts that appear on his path, Jales Coutinho fortifies love as a curriculum theorist must: "I deliberatively engage and juxtapose scholarly texts and promulgate *care/giving* in the unfolding of autobiographies to support calls for reconciliation with self, alterity, nature, and the cosmos." Like Walt Whitman, Jales Coutinho contains "multitudes."[10]

Among the contributions this text makes is "the tracing of the intrinsic connection between love as an ethics of care/giving, autobiography, law, and reconciliation for the unfolding of curriculum in Post-Reconceptualization," positioning "reconciliation" as *the* pinnacle of curriculum conceived as a "collective public moral enterprise." Jales Coutinho reconstructs reconciliation as an "praxis for becoming *consciente* (and loving) in the world," rehabilitates relationships as "respectful," affirming "iterative and symbiotic processes of giving and receiving *from within*, which can ultimately enact a new form of power sharing in the world." Such "work from within," he continues, "sets *the tone* of complicated conversations towards justice and, within justice, reconciliation." And tone turns into "mindsets and attitudes in our collective engagement with alterity in the hierarchical, antagonistic, and agonistic structures of societies, especially (neo)liberal ones." Jales Coutinho explains:

> Reconciliation is conceived as a *state of becoming* wherein people from all walks of life *collectively* transform their bellicose ways and shift their "judgementalities" to fortify love *and* depart their complicated conversations from that very nexus of love—caring for and about "self," "alterity," "nature," and the whole "cosmos."

Reconciled, each of us can contain "multitudes" too.

Turns out there are multitudes of meanings of love hidden in the intellectual history of Curriculum Studies. Jales Coutinho excavates these too, framing his efforts as enactments of "Post/Reconceptualist method/ology," emphasizing the "employment of juxtapositions," by means of which he seeks "understanding(s)" that nourish "*nexus.*" He does so by working his way through the scholarly "literature produced by scholars within and outside curriculum studies to juxtapose interpretations and meanings," thereby composing "a new synoptic text," one that depicts "*the way we go about loving* in curriculum work." Significantly, "rather [than] ... a rupture with the 1970s 'Reconceptualization' ... this 'Post-Reconceptualist' text opens up space for 'complicated conversations' regarding love within and across the con(texts)."

From these labors of love Jales Coutinho concludes that "care" is that which "brings our work together as a collective endeavor in Post-Reconceptualization and internationalization—shifting our labor of love from negotiation towards *proliferation.*" Such "proliferation" performs love as "nexus," a concept that is not only personal but also profoundly political. As Che Guevara knew, "the true revolutionary is guided by strong feelings of love."[11] Such solidarity across difference enables, Jales Coutinho explains, "the fortification of love through the unfolding of autobiography," underscoring that subjectivity is "the real site of education, a praxis for becoming (loving) and *consciente* in the world." As he did in *Curriculum Work and Social Justice Leadership in a Post-Reconceptualist Era: Attaining Critical Consciousness and Learning to Become*, in this text, too, Jales Coutinho performs such praxis autobiographically—and theoretically.

Invoking another term central to his emerging *oeuvre*, Jales Coutinho tells us that "I not only 'bifocalize' my 'self' and 'work' to uncover circuits of privilege and oppression in the course of running—the systems of power that shape(d) my life *and* the lives of those with whom I (have) consciously and unconsciously relate(d)—but also to fortify the meanings of love in my life, relationally and contextually." Through such exegetical excavation he finds he is able "to reaffirm love, the ethics of care, in my life." He speaks of parental love, brotherly love, religious love, romantic love, and labor love, and in so doing forges "nexus" and "proximity" with his "self" and "others." "Because all curriculum work is autobiographical"—indeed the very "heart of education"—Jales Coutinho knows that "the hard labor of fortification (and reconciliation) is best conceived through the unfolding of written, spoken, and performative autobiographical lexis." Such self-disclosure enables each of us "to fortify love, collectively, to give care *from within.*"

Foreword xiii

"I write this text," Jales Coutinho emphasizes, "thinking of love and of my own autobiographical encounters in the world to inspire new becomings." He knows what he's up against: "Despite good levels of criticality, full skepticism should not dominate the shapes and colors of our hearts." Indeed, he recognizes "the decay of love as the most profound crisis of curriculum." Even when we're unable to offer courses on love, we can aspire to offer whatever course we teach with love. "After all," he reminds, "the educational significance that we nurture with love, the ethics of care/giving, is intrinsically educational: it is purely an educational experience *as lived*." He concludes:

> Running and dwelling, we put our hearts in the front line of our daily actions, in every step we take in the course and on that bridge, mobilizing "the what" (knowledge) so that "the way" (the course) becomes less like a locus for "judicious interpretation," and more like a nexus for relational and contextual encounters: a locus for/of love and reconciliation, a place for self and collective awakening, a nexus for new becomings.

In this world of intensifying emotional inequality, Jales Coutinho's heartfelt affirmation of love constitutes "knowledge of most worth."

Notes

1. Brooks 2022, October 28, A24.
2. Jales Coutinho's characterization. Unless indicated otherwise, all quoted passages come from this text.
3. Brooks 2022, October 28, A24.
4. Ibid.
5. Ibid.
6. Canadians rank eleventh in surveys of world happiness: https://www.tamarackcommunity.ca/latest/are-canadians-happy
7. Brooks 2022, October 28, A24.
8. Ibid.
9. Jales Coutinho concludes "that if we are going to teach students about religions, we should attempt to teach them about how religions approach and teach care, how we can become more caring towards our 'selves' and our 'neighbors' within and beyond our own religion, in our own spirituality, whilst minimizing divisions to promote some convergence, to reverberate love within *and* beyond schools." Such a curriculum might communicate—even for the secular—the centrality of love—of care—in subjective and social reconstruction.
10. https://poets.org/poem/song-myself-51
11. https://globaljusticecenter.org/papers/che-guevara%E2%80%99s-concept-revolutionary-love

References

Brooks, D. (2022, October 28). The rising tide of global sadness. *The New York Times*, CLXXII, No. 59, 590, A24.

Macdonald, B. J. (Ed.) (1995). *Theory as a prayerful act: The collected essays of James B. Macdonald*. Peter Lang.

Acknowledgments

Every time I step out of the door which is my self, I am asked to meet someone's else hospitality, but it seems that I have lost my own, for I can no longer give with a full heart. I now wonder what has been left of my humanity: *Will the course ever be able to gift it back to me?* At this historical juncture, I do not think so. My only option then is to try to change it by seeking and studying, by returning to genesis, to love.

Indeed, despite the course, love has been a companion, for I am a believer. Even though I may not remember the love of inception, I have felt the love unfold in the form of motherhood and fatherhood care. I have greeted love in the eyes of a some people and, later, in letters, words, and cartoons of appreciation, in hugs of friendship, and in the glories of nature, too.

For all those who paved a way, for all those who continue to help me overcome adversities, reach to my dreams, and see the meaning of life as unfolding lexis from a fortified nexus of love: To Mom, Dad, family, friends, and other lifelong caregivers, among them teachers, therapists, as well as curricularists who care for and about the multiple and intersecting con(texts) in schools. To all my scholarly connections and those who gifted their time to contribute to my scholarship, including Routledge blind reviewers and editors—and to dear Bill (who always asks groundbreaking questions and incentivizes me to study)—all the love which I can give, as it unfolds in these divisive times, attempting to forge and fortify nexus and proximity.

1 Introduction

This text is a text of love and fortification; a text that calls upon curricularists to advance Post-Reconceptualization as a "collective public moral enterprise" in democratic institutions as a lexis and praxis of/for love and reconciliation, in both global north and global south contexts.

Following the post-reconceptualist tenets proposed in *Curriculum work and social justice leadership in a post-reconceptualist era: attaining critical consciousness and learning to become* (henceforth: CWSJL), curricularists have been called upon to: (i) bifocalize "self" and "work" in running the course of development and (ii) disrupt "single thoughts" in education; (iii) confront fears associated with such disruptions; (iv) forge and (v) fortify a "nexus" of love from which to depart complicated conversations; and (vi) work across differences, refusing "denials" and "talking with," while (vii) overcoming dangers, thus promoting "nexus" and "proximity" in a divisive and conflictuous world of becoming(s). This text aims to advance the *fifth* post-reconceptualist tenet of curriculum work: **the fortification of love**. To fortify love, I deliberatively engage and juxtapose scholarly texts and promulgate *care/giving* in the unfolding of autobiographies to support calls for reconciliation with self, alterity, nature, and the cosmos.

One of the greatest contributions of this text regards the tracing of the intrinsic connection between love as an ethics of care/giving, autobiography, law, and reconciliation for the unfolding of curriculum in post-reconceptualization. Although "reconciliation" conveys different messages to individuals positioned in various intersections across the large spectrum of diversity, this text perceives reconciliation as *the* pinnacle of curriculum work as a "collective public moral enterprise." Inspired in the concept of the Truth and Reconciliation Commission of Canada (TRC) (2015) and in the deliberations encountered in CWSJL and in other post-reconceptualist texts (e.g. Côté et al., 2021;

DOI: 10.4324/9781003359968-1

2 Introduction

Datta, 2020; du Preez, 2014), I conceive reconciliation as an evolving phenomena—a lexis and praxis for becoming *consciente* (and loving) in the world—, the forging of mutually respectful relationships culminating in and from iterative and symbiotic processes of given and receiving *from within*, which can ultimately enact a new form of energy and power sharing in the world.

Conceived in the unfolding of autobiography (the course of running—and the bridges— from where people come to "dwell," "run," "bifocalize" and "talk with," from a fortified nexus of love), the *lexis* that culminates from relational *and* contextual autobiographical understanding(s) can ultimately transform our *praxis* through our "critical agencies." Such "work from within" (Pinar, 1972) sets *the tone* of complicated conversations towards justice and, within justice, reconciliation. Indeed, "working from within while looking outwards" (Jales Coutinho, 2022) conceives reconciliation as lexis *and* praxis of/for becoming *consciente* (Freire, 1970) and loving in the world: subject and social (re)construction that culminates in the change of mindsets and attitudes in our collective engagement with alterity in the hierarchical, antagonistic, and agonistic structures of societies, especially (neo)liberal ones. Reconciliation is conceived as a *state of becoming* wherein people from all walks of life *collectively* transform their bellicose ways and shift their "judgementalities" to fortify love *and* depart their complicated conversations from that very nexus of love—caring for and about "self," "alterity," "nature," and the whole "cosmos."

In CWSJL, I alluded to the fact that scholars have studied and theorized the "standpoints" of love, hospitality, and solidarity within and outside curriculum studies including, but not limited to, bell hooks, Rubén-Gaztambide Fernández, Jack Miller, Kathleen Gallagher, Tom Popkewitz, Liesa Griffin Smith, Molly Quinn, Nathan Snaza, and William H. Schubert. Running the course *of* development, I discerned experiences with the standpoints of hospitality and solidarity in an antagonistic, agonistic, competitive, and hierarchical world of becoming(s). The running of the course helped me differentiate the ways through which individuals have engaged with "hospitality" and "solidarity" in the world, which ultimately culminated a "nexus of love" commenced on *care*. By running the course, I argued that individuals can become "hospitable" and receive alterity in their midst and exert "solidarities" because they have invested interests in a relationship and hope to sustain, for example, a "servant-served paradigm" (Hooks, 1994, p. 103). In other words, individuals may engage with hospitality and solidarity from a standpoint other than love, thus exempting the ethical and moral commitments to care for and about dignity, wellbeing, and flourishing—all of which command short- and long-term care towards self and alterity. This commitment to dwell in love aims to reduce *and* eradicate vulnerabilities, suffering, and unjust power differentials in the world.

Because of hierarchization and unprincipled competition, people may be inclined to position love as make-believe and perceive caregiving as an unconceivable lexis for becoming in (neo)liberalism. As I have pointed out in CWSJL, when love is questioned and deconstructed through criticality in the (neo)liberal state, other practices and meanings such as bitterness and hatred can end up constituting our collective unfolding. In this book, I argue that such predicament makes the intertwined endeavours of *studying* love (the academic undertaking of understanding in post/reconceptualization) and *fortifying* love (the praxis of reasserting care/giving in our midst and in the unfolding of autobiographies) crucial for curriculum and education generally. In CWSJL, I argued that "love as concept and sentiment [had already] been the center of many debates within and outside religious and academic circles in both global-north and -south contexts" (Jales Coutinho, 2022, p. 37). Without engaging or entertaining such meanings, I espoused the *one* meaning that constituted the center of the "nexus" from which curricularists were invited to depart their complicated conversations: gift-love, or love-as-genesis, the willingness to give care while receiving vulnerability in return—that is, giving and receiving *from within*. This willingness to give care, regardless of whether someone receives something "valuable" in exchange, I associated with an "ethics of care" in curriculum.

In this **first critical moment** towards *fortification*, I continue to acknowledge that scholars and curricularists have attributed several meanings to the concept of "love," which may or may not intersect with care/giving. But, instead of just acknowledging diversity in thought, I unfold this text to *re*engage my "self" with curriculum studies. A study conceptualized through a post/reconceptualist method/ology, the employment of juxtapositions, I foster understanding(s) and promote *nexus*. I deliberately engage with the literature produced by scholars within and outside curriculum studies to juxtapose interpretations and meanings—in this case, meanings related to love and situated in the "vertical" and "horizontal" structures of the discipline, the intellectual histories and present circumstances constituted of social, political, and intellectual milieus (see Pinar, 2007, p. xiv)—to unfold a new synoptic text for curriculum. In other words, this text aims to describes *the way we go about loving* in curriculum work.

Rather than deconstructing or comparing meanings attributed to love as a "curriculum concept," the juxtaposition offers an *understanding* of "love" embedded and situated in the contextual relations of appreciation, desire, understanding, compassion etc. which have emerged in the course *of* development and constituted curriculum work prior and after "post-reconceptualist" discourses, including meanings that have been (re)produced in the midst of post-reconceptualist "internationalization" (See Gough, 2000; Pinar, 2008, 2013; Trueit et al., 2003). I continue to espouse the proposition that "post-reconceptualization" is a movement/moment "opened up to play, contestations, and as of yet unknown meanings" (Malewski, 2010, p. xiii) which unfolds in conversation among several generations of curriculum workers: people who labor in the nexus of theory, policy, and practice to articulate, circulate, (de)construct, evaluate, facilitate, interpret, implement, translate, proliferate, (re)present, and understand curriculum work, etc. Curriculum work constitutes a site of/for "playfulness" of which *complicated conversations* are its cornerstone, the very *character* of curriculum studies—subjective, social, communicative, cosmopolitan (see Pinar, 2011)—and whose setting of tone can forge a path towards justice.

Indeed, with a preoccupation geared towards *understanding*, this text follows the long-standing *reconceptualist* tradition of "understanding curriculum" (Pinar, 2008). Through juxtaposition, this text attempts to connect "past" and "present" understanding(s) into a coherent "nexus" from which "proximity" can be attained (Jales Coutinho, 2022, p. 51). I depart from the premise that the study of love as a standpoint/subject of/for curriculum through juxtaposition—when emerging from an intellectual commitment *to understand* alterity *and* the course itself "as a whole"—can be paramount for *fortification* (the praxis of reasserting care/giving in the unfolding of our autobiographies) and reconciliation (the lexis and praxis of becoming in the world). By juxtaposing how curricularists have employed this curricular concept in their work, I connect meaning(s) to forge a tentative and yet ever-expansive "whole." Hence, rather than suggesting a rupture with "Reconceptualization" (Pinar, 1978), this "Post-Reconceptualist" text opens up space for "complicated conversations" regarding love within and across con(texts).

By reaching a climax in my study of love through juxtapositions, I *re*state, in a **second critical moment**, the meaning of love as an ethics of care/giving in curriculum work. "Care" has been paramount to post-reconceptualization (see, for example, Burns, 2018) and for my own "nexus of love" grounded on the standpoints of love, hospitality, and solidarity. However, like "love" itself, the concept of "care" is rife with multiplicities of meanings (and actions) (see, for example, Noddings, 2013). *The way we go about caring* in our daily encounters differs among individuals, groups, communities, and nation-states. Caring for and about "self" and "others" is indeed a "complicated conversation," a labor akin to seekers, a site where divergencies and convergences occur. At this critical juncture, I shed light on Ted Aoki's "bridge" to underscore the needed connection that curriculum work has to make with love as an ethics of care/giving while offering another reading on love-as-genesis through the discussion of hierarchy, power, capability, and difference. The pivotal connection between curriculum work and care, shaped by the spellbinding work of curricularists such as Jung-Hoon Jung (2016), is paramount to this quest of/for becoming. Indeed, I argue that "care" is what brings our work together as a collective endeavour in Post-Reconceptualization and internationalization—shifting our labor of love from negotiation towards *proliferation*, turning encounters with care/giving *from within* less probabilistic in the course.

Recognizing the decay of love as the most profound crisis of curriculum, attuned to the divergences attributed to "care," and mindful of possible conflicts that such incongruences can elicit in the daily encounters with the (un)known, this text attempts to uncover some of the meanings that have been attributed to love as an ethics of care/giving in education. Because of possible discrepancies in meanings, I dedicate part of this text to "divergencies and convergences." From divergence, I invite curricularists to forge "convergence in divergencies" as an opportunity to conceive "nexus" and bolster "fortification" in curriculum work. As I have alluded in CWSJL, we live in a paradoxical world full of complexities that can only exist because of divergencies. Yet, we should always strive to seek "the whole" and build convergences from divergencies as we run the course of complicated conversations *in* development.

While "study" in the form of juxtaposition offered an opportunity to forge a vertical and horizontal understanding of love in curriculum "as nexus," the "study" that I offer in a **third critical moment** is conceptualized as "the real site of education" (Pinar, 2015, p. 14), the mobilization of academic knowledge/theories in the threading of one's autobiography (see Pinar, 2011, 2015, 2019). Pinar devised and, with the support of Madeleine R. Grumet, crafted *currere* as an autobiographical educational method which aimed to disclose "the inner lived experiences of external structures" (Pinar & Grumet, 1976, p. xii) through four steps: the regressive, progressive, analytical, and synthetic moments. In CWSJL, I espoused a post-reconceptualist account of autobiography by turning "critical bifocality" (Weis & Fine, 2012) into a verb: to "bifocalize." By "seeking contexts" (Greene, 1995) whilst mobilizing academic knowledge to bifocalize "self" and "work" in regressive, progressive, analytical and synthetical moments in the course *of* development, one facilitates the attainment of greater levels of *conscientização*—the lexis and praxis of "learning to become" in the world.

Whereas the first account of "study" espoused in this text favoured juxtaposition, the second account of "study" as the real site of education turns this post-reconceptualist conversation into an ongoing proposition for curricularists to dedicate "curriculum studies" to the *fortification of love* through the unfolding of autobiography—at least if we are to accomplish the *collective* project of post-reconceptualization in internationalization. Indeed, this third critical moment offers an opportunity to unfold the autobiographical con(text) as the real site of education, a praxis for becoming (loving) and *consciente* in the world. In CWSJL, I alluded to the fact that my short autobiographical account about *conscientização* was concise and that I could "envisage a longer one, which might occur via another project" (Jales Coutinho, 2022, p. 89). I take this opportunity to unfold a much longer autobiographical account of becoming in my study.

Running the course regressively, progressively, analytically, and synthetically, I "bifocalize" my "self" and "work" not only to uncover circuits of privilege and oppression in the course of running—the systems of power that shape(d) my life *and* the lives of those with whom I (have) consciously and unconsciously relate(d)—, but also to fortify the meanings of love in my life, relationally and contextually. In other words, I unfold my autobiographical lexis to reaffirm love, the ethics of care/giving, in my life. I speak about parental love, brotherhood love, religious love, romantic love, and labor love, forging "nexus" and "proximity" with my "self" and "others" in these increasingly divisive times. I run the course and engage in subject (re)construction, mobilizing academic knowledge from texts published in several fields, including the fields of psychology and religious studies, to advance the work of post-reconceptualization in schools, research institutions, and policy circles. Because all curriculum work can be considered autobiographical (Cooper & White, 2012; Taliaferro-Baszile, 2010), and because it constitutes "the heart of education" (Jales Coutinho, 2022, p. 161), I contend that curricularists can better achieve the hard labor of fortification (and reconciliation) through the unfolding of written, spoken, and performative autobiographical lexis.

Much (more) could be written about the labor of love, but as I unfold my relational and contextual autobiographical lexis, I also become (more) cognizant of the fact that autobiographies need to unfold as *relational* encounters, locally and globally (Evans, 2002), within and across con(texts). Although I could attempt to advance this project in solitude by writing hundreds of pages on the subject of love (e.g. as in religious love), I know that this constitutes a *collective* enterprise, one that I aspire to build *with* others. As a matter of fact, this is one of the reasons I have constructed curriculum as a "public moral enterprise" (Gaztambide-Fernández & Sears, 2004) very much a *collective* project.

Indeed, I strongly believe that other curricularists placed in various positions across the spectrum of diversity are better positioned to advance certain parts of this text and contribute to the relational, contextual, and paradoxical "whole" of curriculum. Moreover, due to my social positioning as a White-passing Latino and queer scholar, the meanings that I uncover in my autobiography might look pedestrian and not fully comprise the "care" that we may encounter in communities and societies across all corners of the world. Yet, as in my first work about post-reconceptualization, I hope my autobiographical lexis elicits relational *and* contextual understanding(s), connecting my "self" with alterity, including individuals who reside in non-Western con(texts).

In a **fourth critical moment**, I turn this complicated conversation to the intersection of education and law—an intersection which becomes materialized in institutionalized *evaluations*, the very course of running *in* development. As I hope to clarify in this text, when speaking of reconciliation, one has to turn one's attention to evaluations, and to the institution of education and law, for both contribute to shaping the phenomena of reconciliation in schools (and beyond). Within education and law, I highlight how each institution approaches and shapes the phenomena of reconciliation in the large scene of life, be it in schools or in the courts. I draw reflections about generalizations, love, and justice, and discern some of the position(s) that evaluations have enjoyed in societies at large through the institution of law and education in (neo) liberal democracy. Moreover, I underscore that evaluations have become an intrinsic object of "governmentality" (Foucault, 2009, p. 108), often halting love and reconciliation in the hierarchies of becoming and in the unfolding of autobiographies. Therefore, I call upon curricularists to attribute other meanings to this object of governmentality, drawing attention to the quest of becoming *consciente* (and loving) in the world. Here, I attempt to answer how internal, external, and self-evaluations can (or cannot) support "actualization" and a new world where our situatedness of becoming supplants "judgementalities" for "subjectivementalities" in the course of running. Once again, I purposefully employ the autobiographical con(text) to connect my own experience with the complicated world of evaluations and schooling, and to provide insights for educators and policymakers, too.

In a **concluding moment**, I briefly write about the intrinsic connection between love and reconciliation. Perhaps too eager to run the course and unable to see the hidden (and not-so-hidden) contours of our labor as these unfold in a fast-paced globalized world, communities of scholars, practitioners, and policymakers may not always savour the labor of reconciliation in the hierarchies in which they live and work. I borrow the words of James Colin Field (2018) to invite curricularists to "begin in love" (p. 47) as they labor, continuously, to forge a nexus of theory, policy, and practice while "expanding the sphere of critical educational efforts at each of these levels" (Apple, 2018, p. 685), setting the tone of complicated conversations towards *justice*.

This book's key premise lays out the fortification of love, collectively, to give care *from within*. We can only achieve this labor of love and reconciliation, of post-reconceptualization, when we start to think consciously about each and every connection we make in the course—with "self," "alterity," "nature," and the "cosmos"—by critically asking: ***Can we build a world where love is not negotiated, but only proliferated?***

Such fortification and the proliferation of love may lead *us* to a place where educators, students, administrators, and policymakers everywhere—including my own relational and contextual "self"—have an opportunity to continue unfold(ing) their autobiographies, attaining greater levels of *conscientização*, from a fortified nexus of love, towards justice (and reconciliation) in the course *of* development: a labor that can transcend one's own lifetime.

Love in the Post-Reconceptualist Era of Curriculum Work: Deliberations on the Meanings of Care comprises five interconnected essays where I advance the fifth tenet of curriculum as a collective public moral enterprise—the fortification of love—so that we can aspire to build *and* share a future across differences in increasingly divisive times.

References

Apple, M. W. (2018). Critical curriculum studies and the concrete problems of curriculum policy and practice. *Journal of Curriculum Studies, 50*(6), 685–690. https://doi.org/10.1080/00220272.2018.1537373

Burns, J. P. (2018). *Power, curriculum, and embodiment: Re-thinking curriculum as counter-conduct and counter-politics*. Palgrave Macmillan.

Cooper, K., & White, R. E. (2012). *Qualitative research in the post-modern era: Contexts of qualitative research*. Springer Netherlands.

Introduction 9

Côté, R., Denis, J., Watts, V., & Wilkes, R. (2021). Indigenization, institutions, and imperatives: Perspectives on reconciliation from the CSA Decolonization Sub-Committee. *Canadian Review of Sociology/Revue Canadienne De Sociologie*, *58*(1), 105–117. https://doi.org/10.1111/cars.12325

Datta, R. (2020). Indigenous reconciliation: Why, what, and how. *International Journal of Critical Indigenous Studies*, *12*(2), 47–63. https://doi.org/10.5204/ijcis.v12i2.1276

du Preez, P. (2014). Reconciliation through dialogical nostalgia in post-conflict societies: A curriculum to intersect *Compare: A Journal of Comparative International Education*, *44*(1), 117–135. https://doi.org/10.1080/03057925.2013.859875

Evans, K. M. (2002). *Negotiating the self: identity, sexuality, and emotion in learning to teach*. RoutledgeFalmer.

Field, J. C. (2018). Curriculum in the post truth era: Is truth dead? *Canadian Social Studies*, *50*(2), 44–48. https://doi.org/10.29173/css15

Foucault, M. (2009). *Michel foucault: Security, territory, population. Lectures at the collège de France, 1977–1978*. (G. Burchell, & M. Senellart, Ed.). Palgrave Macmillan.

Freire, P. (1970). *Pedagogy of the oppressed*. Continuum.

Gaztambide-Fernández, R. A., & Sears, J. T. (Eds.). (2004). *Curriculum work as a public moral enterprise*. Rowman & Littlefield Publishers.

Gough, N. (2000). Locating curriculum studies in the Global Village. *Journal of Curriculum Studies*, *32*(2), 329–342. https://doi.org/10.1080/002202700182790

Greene, M. (1995). *Releasing the imagination: Essays on education, the arts, and social change*. Jossey-Bass Publishers.

hooks, b. (1994). *Teaching to transgress: Education as the practice of freedom*. Routledge.

Jales Coutinho, A. M. (2022). *Curriculum work and social justice leadership in a post-reconceptualist era: Attaining critical consciousness and learning to become* (1st ed.). Routledge. https://doi.org/10.4324/9781003188629

Jung, J. (2016). *The concept of care in curriculum studies: Juxtaposing Currere and Hakbeolism*. Routledge.

Malewski, E. (2010). *Curriculum studies handbook: The next moment*. Routledge.

Noddings, N. (2013). *Caring: A relational approach to ethics and moral education* (2nd ed.). University of California Press.

Pinar, W. F. (1972, January). Working from within. *Educational Leadership*, *29*(4), 329–331.

Pinar, W. F. (1978). The reconceptualization of curriculum studies. *Journal of Curriculum Studies*, *10*(3), 205–214.

Pinar, W. F. (2007). *Intellectual advancement through disciplinarity: Verticality and horizontality in curriculum*. Sense.

Pinar, W. F. (2008). Curriculum theory since 1950: Crisis, reconceptualization, internationalization. In F. M. Connelly, M. F. He, & J. Phillion (Eds.), *The SAGE handbook of curriculum and instruction* (pp. 491–513). Sage.

Pinar, W. F. (2011). *The character of curriculum studies: Bildung, currere, and the recurring question of the subject*. Palgrave Macmillan.

Pinar, W. F. (Ed.). (2013). *International handbook of curriculum research* (2nd ed.). Routledge. https://doi.org/10.4324/9780203831694

Pinar, W. F. (2015). *Educational experience as lived: Knowledge, history, alterity: The selected works of William F. Pinar*. Routledge.

Pinar, W. F. (2019). *What is curriculum theory?* (3rd ed.). Routledge.

Pinar, W. F., & Grumet, M. R. (1976). *Toward a poor curriculum*. Kendall & Hunt.

Taliaferro-Baszile, D. (2010). In ellisonian eyes, what is curriculum theory? In E. Malewski (Ed.). *Curriculum studies handbook: The next moment* (pp. 483–495). Routledge.

The Truth and Reconciliation Commission of Canada. (2015). *Honouring the truth, reconciling for the future: Summary of the final report of the truth and reconciliation commission of Canada*. The Government of Canada.

Trueit, D., Doll, W. E., Wang, H., & Pinar, W. F. (Eds.). (2003). *The internationalization of curriculum studies: Selected proceedings from the Lsu conference 2000*. Peter Lang.

Weis, L., & Fine, M. (2012). Critical bifocality and circuits of privilege: Expanding critical ethnographic theory and design. *Harvard Educational Review,82*(2),173–201.https://doi.org/10.17763/haer.82.2.v1jx34n441532242

2 Studying love through juxtapositions in curriculum

Where to begin this course if not in love? I commence this text hoping to unfold a relational and contextual lexis from my study, to fortify and proliferate love, however difficult this quest may be, as we run, collectively, the complicated and troubling course *of* development.

Before engaging in the *unfolding* of autobiography as the "very site of education" (Pinar, 2011, p. xiii)—the study which occurs, in solitude and with others, through the mobilization of academic knowledge in the threading of subjectivity in autobiography—, I direct my study to "juxtapositions," a concept employed by several curricularists in this complexifying and troubling era for curriculum studies. Generally speaking, juxtaposition means to "put things that are not similar next to each other" (Cambridge Dictionary, 2008, p. 783). In the field of Curriculum Studies, "juxtapositions" have embodied similar meanings and shaped the work of curricularists including, but not limited to, Janet Miller (2005) and William F. Pinar (2009).

For example, in *Curriculum Studies Handbook: The Next Moment*, Erik Malewski (2010) employed "juxtaposition" to connect "the work of newer academicians who offer[ed] fresh perspectives *in relation to* essays from longtime scholars who reveal[ed] the historic and current motivations for their intellectual work" (p. xi; emphasis added). The juxtapositions allowed curricularists to work from within and create, together, novel accounts on curriculum con(texts). Most recently, other curricularists have employed juxtapositions among con(texts)/ methods, too. The South Korean curricularist Jung-Hoon Jung (2016) employed the juxtaposition of *currere* with 'Hakbeolism'—a Korean concept related to experiences with 'cultural capital' generated and produced by the hierarchical and prestigious systems of tertiary institutions (p. 2)—in order to study: the (i) historical formation of Korean test-score system (historical and institutional contexts); and (ii) self-understanding via *currere* (autobiographical context), articulating such understanding(s) through an ethics of care in curriculum studies.

Likewise, the Canadian curricularist Teresa Strong-Wilson (2021) has related the term "juxtaposition" to the word "coincidence" (p. 7), "putting into relation or 'Benjaminian constellation' elements from disparate contexts" (Strong-Wilson, 2021, p. 13). Conceived as a "mode of bringing disparate things, people, events intro provocative *relation*, even as these also remain distinct from one another" (Strong-Wilson, 2021, p. 23; emphasis added), Strong-Wilson argues that juxtapositions support curriculum's "ethical self-encounters" (Strong-Wilson, 2021, p. 23), which directly involve the unfolding of autobiography as the real site of education (Strong-Wilson, 2021)— that is, the transformation of *implicated* subjects into *concerned* ones. Finally, I think it is fair to say that I have also offered a juxtaposition of *currere* with "critical bifocality" (Weis & Fine, 2012) when I turned the latter into a verb in CWSJL: to bifocalize "self" and "work" in the course of running in development (Jales Coutinho, 2022).

In a personal exchange with Pinar, he underscored the increasing presence of "juxtapositions" in the field of curriculum studies. From this conversation, I began to recognize that juxtapositions have become an increasingly powerful tool in the art of understanding *and* (re)constructing curriculum as a "course of study" and also a "course of running." Juxtaposition supports the mapping of con(texts) that have emerged and proliferated in the field, and has transformed the enterprise when curricularists are able to forge *and* uncover hidden and not-so-hidden *relations* among such con(texts) (e.g. material relations often translated in power relations, that is, relations of domination and subordination, as well as the relations of love, care, and friendship that can be gifted in the course of development etc.). In other words, juxtapositions induce the searching of material and discursive con(texts) of which curriculum are made of, forging and uncovering relations—the "seeking" proposed by Maxine Greene in her quest to see the world "big" (Greene, 1995, pp. 10–16). So, in a way, juxtapositions have become a **mode of inquiry**, a form of study that can espouse con(textual) *relations* by "enabling [a] focus on the distinctiveness of difference, the primacy of particularity, all the while affirming their *relationality*" (Pinar, 2016, p. 196; emphasis added).

By *understanding* curriculum in its multiple forms as an object and subject, its intellectual, con(textual) histories and its present circumstances "locally and globally" (Pinar, 2006, p. 163), we can also deconstruct it, and rewrite it, and, in playfulness, bring the "vertical" and "horizontal" structures of the discipline (Pinar, 2007) together, even if tentatively, into "a whole," that is, into a *nexus* (Jales Coutinho, 2022, p. 51). Here, I argue that when we juxtapose con(texts) *relationally* as a form of study, we can forge a nexus of understanding across differences that can provide a more expansive form of knowledge, understanding, co-creation, and transformation for curriculum—an understanding that can culminate into new progressions for the course itself. Indeed, to the extent that juxtapositions bring con(texts) together to enhance our understanding of curriculum as it unfolds, continuously and paradoxically, in/as/for/and against the course *of* development, they also promote vital understanding(s) for the *real* site of education: when curricularists *explicitly* bring into their juxtapositions the autobiographical con(text) (aka. *currere*) to mobilize critical and powerful knowledge (including other life narratives and knowledge from academic disciplines) to thread and bifocalize the "self" in regressive, progressive, analytical, and synthetical moments in the course *of* development, and, through running, elicit relational *and* con(textual) autobiographical understanding(s).

At this critical juncture, I juxtapose texts to *understand curriculum* locally and globally, seeking to comprehend the meanings and discourses attributed to the concept of love and which have circulated this objectified subject and subjectified object. I invite curricularists to run this course, however incomplete it may seem, and to dwell with me in the academic study of the following questions: *How has love been conceptualized in curriculum theory, policy, and practice? How has the concept of love been portrayed in/intersected the curriculum field?* While acknowledging that the field has become "expansive, producing scholarly landscape that is often difficult to grasp and nearly impossible to survey" (Gaztambide-Fernández, 2009, p. 250), I do attempt to situate this text within the "vertical" and "horizontal" structures of curriculum studies (Pinar, 2007), exploring the histories and the present circumstances of the discipline *in relation to the concept of love*. As stated by Pinar (2016): "The disciplinary conversation is constantly changing, but intellectual advancement requires that we link what has been said before *alongside*—in *relation* to—present preoccupations [and future prospects]" (p. 200, emphasis in original).

Recognizing increasing concerns that "those who try to make sense of the present confusion by reference to the past rarely go beyond the emergence of the curriculum field as a profession in North America" (Egan, 2003, p. 10), I humbly expand my search to seek a multitude of con(texts) from those "present and absent, contemporaries but also the dead and, [even if paradoxically], those not yet born" (Pinar, 2016,

p. xi). In seeking, I attempt to forge a collective understanding of *love* within and across con(texts). I present juxtapositions in a circularly-chronological manner (juxtaposing texts chronologically, but returning to them whenever necessary), however incomplete and imperfect this project may be from the very outset. But fear of incompletion does not deter me: I share hooks's (2000) concern that a shared understanding of love—at least an intersectional one—is necessary if we are to "create love" (p. 11), or, as proposed in this book, to fortify it.

By situating this text within and across the "vertical" and the "horizontal," locally and globally, I also look for the third dimension: a progression, a futurity that envisions novel prospects for this field under the seven Post-Reconceptualist tenets of curriculum work as a "collective public moral enterprise," in particular, the fortification of love.

2.1 The way we go about loving: understanding "love" in curriculum, within and across con(texts)

In the aftermath of the "reconceptualist movement" in the 1970's in the United States, curricularists have attempted to understand curriculum as historical con(text), and, in the process, to (re)search the origins of the enterprise. In *Understanding curriculum*, William Pinar et al. (1995) argued that many curricularists have conceived "the birth" of Curriculum Studies with Franklin Bobbitt's (1918) publication of *The Curriculum* (Pinar et al., 1995, p. 70). However, with the emergence of the internationalization of the field (See Pinar, 2008), it has become evident that the word *curriculum* has been employed in an "educational sense" for many centuries now, as the object of several conceptualizations, in both global-north and -south con(texts) (see Jung & Pinar, 2016).

For example, many curricularists conceive the enterprise not only as a "course of study," but also as the "running of the course" (Deng, 2018, p. 694). Produced, positioned, and interpreted both as an object and a subject, encountered in historical documents and con(textual) discourses, "alive in culture and language" (Malewski, 2010, p. 11), as well as in "juxtapositions" that also highlight the "distinctiveness of difference" (Pinar, 2016, p. 196) and in "nexus" that forges "proximity" (Jales Coutinho, 2022), the "curriculum-as-plan" and the "curriculum-as-lived" (Aoki, 1986/1991/2005) have become an entity, a phenomena, an outcome, a course and an event, the playful composition of unfolding lexis and praxis in and for education—that is, a "complicated conversation" (Wals et al., 2022) whose multifaceted con(texts) are forever intertwined in past, present, and future articulations culminating in theoretical, practical, and critical policy concerns and propositions (Apple, 2018), locally and worldly (Pinar, 2016).

Throughout the course of development and since its "birth," curriculum has invited "love" to constitute and transform lexis and praxis. As Erik Gleibermann (2016) reminds us, "love" is an ancient lexis: Plato's *The Symposium* and his understanding of *eros*, *philia*, and *agape* might be one of the earliest Westernized philosophical scholarly expressions of "love." But looking closer to the field of "curriculum" as a contemporary "event" rather than the "course of development" itself, we are invited to peruse the work of curricularists such as Franklin Bobbit—people who provided building blocks for the "event" we recognize as the school curriculum, the object that constitutes "the course" of one's study in schools. Known for his devotion to efficiency and eugenicist ideas (Bobbitt, 1909, 1912), Bobbitt dedicated part of his curriculum work to love too, albeit a "love" of a different kind: love as "admiration" and "devotion" to a place (Moore, 2015). In *The Curriculum*, Bobbitt (1918) described and compared what constituted "the good citizen" (p. 117) in "primitive tribes" (p. 119) and in the "modern situation" (p. 120). Patriotism, he argued, was one of "the characteristic of the good citizen" (Bobbitt, 1918, p. 122).

The desire to serve one's country, the "love of one's people" (p. 123), may be the first meaning ascribed to "love" by Franklin Bobbitt (1918) in curriculum. However, curricularists are constantly reminded of the objectified status ascribed to curriculum as a recipient of knowledge (Grumet et al., 2008). In such a state, the first "love" that might intersect curriculum con(texts) is that of a "love for knowledge," which can be best described as an appreciation for new "understandings," a curiosity and desire for "learning" and "wisdom." A love for knowledge has been upheld, for example, by Charlotte Mason in 1929, a female British educationalist who cherished the role of books while criticizing utilitarian theory and the priority ascribed to psychological concerns in education, which she feared could "eliminate knowledge" (Mason & Mason, 1929, p. 242) from curriculum propositions.

In *Love and compassion: Exploring their role in education*, John P. Miller (2018) qualifies this love as a "state of enthusiasm" (Sean Pidgeon in Miller, 2018, p. 52) which many educationalists consider "the goal of all teaching" (Miller, 2018, p. 52). Writing about research on curiosity (which he qualifies as 'directed' and 'exploratory', 'specific' and 'diverse'), Miller (2018) explains what happens to individuals when they relate with bodies of knowledge in a joyful way, and which conditions may support one's love of learning. Miller (2018) also expounds that schools have deterred such curiosity, a preoccupation that became relevant for progressive educators.

Fostering a "love of learning" becomes a special facet of curriculum work when students struggle to learn content from the disciplines. For example, in such con(texts), educators engage with "love kindness" to show unconditional positive regard for students, inspiring learners to foster a "love for learning" through resilience, value, authentic struggle, and support (see Baker et al., 2019). Often considered a perennial searching for humans in Western and non-Western conceptualizations of curriculum (see Jung & Pinar, 2016—conceptualizations of curriculum e.g. *Gyo-yuk-bon-wi-ron*), the "love of learning" and/or "love of study" has also constituted: (i) a facet of "lifelong discourses" in postmodernity—when not solely focused on 'upskilling' and 'reskilling' (Morgan-Klein & Osborne, 2007) and when employed to measure one's curiosity, engagement and academic aptitude; and (ii) a facet of "deficit narratives" too (see, for example, Valencia, 2020).

While different types of "curiosity" may describe a "love" of learning in curriculum and education, there exist other important conceptualizations that have intersected curriculum con(texts). In *The Lure of the Transcendent: Collected Essays by Dwayne E. Huebner*, Pinar (1999) attested that through the study of aesthetic, phenomenological, political, and theological con(texts), Huebner's scholarship played a pivotal role in the paradigmatic shift of "Reconceptualization." Among the 35 essays included in this volume, 11 addressed matters pertaining to the concept of love in curriculum. Between 1961 and 1963, and then between 1985 and 1987, Huebner provided a conceptualization of "love" grounded on notions of responsibility, care, conversation, and spirituality, the latter been the focus of his scholarship in the 1980's, especially in the study of the theological con(text). Such conceptualization not only attended to knowledge in curriculum, but to relationships, and to the transcendent.

Between 1961 and 1963, Huebner questioned the adequacy of the elementary curriculum. He claimed that the curriculum did not lack knowledge of the world, but rather "responsibility" (Huebner, 1962b, p. 11): "curriculum has not yet found adequate ways to emphasize and to maintain the love and excitement that children have for the world" (p. 13). The most important question, Huebner argued, is whether "we who are living (…) love the world" (p. 11). For Huebner (1961/1999), curiosity was tantamount to responsibility for the world, an enthusiasm that elicited ongoing excitement to sustain our collective existence in the world: "responsibility derives from enthusiastic, joyful participation in the world," claimed Huebner (1961/1999, p. 11). In a second essay, as he advanced his thoughts on the matter, Huebner (1962c/1999) maintained:

> Responsibility for one's own action or for the affairs and state of the world does not begin when a person reaches some age or position. Responsibility is a slowly evolving attitude and awareness, channeled, developed and made more powerful through cultural tools.
>
> (p. 63)

For Huebner (1961/1999), curriculum was not a recipient of knowledge, but rather a "program by which we filter the child's curiosity toward and love for the world" (p. 11) so that the relationship between one's love and one's responsibility for the world unfold.

Huebner (1961/1999) argued that curricularists could evaluate "curriculum in action" (p. 12) by asking, in Nietzsche's words, "*What have you really loved till now?*" (p. 12). Huebner (1961/1999) claimed that "if love ties the self to the rest of the world—caring enough about it, interested enough in it, curious enough about it" (p. 12), then one can ask such questions to help students love the world and "assume responsibility for it" (p. 12). Curriculum content would need to bolster connections between individuals and the world, through both the social and the natural sciences. While curriculum could foster these connections, language would elicit one's imagination through conversation: "Human relationships of conversation and care" (Huebner, 1962a/1999, p. 63) are pivotal, he declared.

Huebner (1962a/1999) posed a second question concerning love and responsibility: "*How may I significantly involve the children in encounters with others, and gradually increase their social responsibility?*" (p. 64). To develop responsibility for self and others, the child must develop "skills of *conversation* and discussion of planning together, of identifying and resolving conflicts, of accepting and carrying through on responsibilities, of criticizing their own efforts and planning ahead" (Huebner, 1962c/1999, p. 64). A classroom needs to be an active space because social action "is the vehicle by which they check their own meanings, become aware of who they are and can be, and help others do the same" (p. 64).

Conversation was paramount to responsibility, and, consequently, to love. For Huebner (1962a/1999), laugher and conversation constituted our shared human condition. Conversation, he argued, was "talking and listening" (p. 68): "it requires a willingness to give of one's self and to receive from the other, and an eagerness to bring the

I and the Thou together in a significant act of relationship and living" (p. 68). He continued: "It is through the give and take of conversation that the child establishes modes of relationship which lead to the give and take of love among equals" (Huebner, 1962/1999, p. 68). Huebner (1963/1999) would classify relationships in four categories and maintained that the exchange of solitude would constitute the "essence of love" (p. 77), for people would seek to exchange and maintain the "maximum freedom of each [individual], (...) freely giv[ing] and receiv[ing] (...), each recogniz[ing] that [one] is alone, separate, but able to give and receive from the other" (p. 76). In Huebner's (1963/1999) account, conversation would constitute a form of love "in action" (p. 78):

> The recipient act on this information, reshape it or himself, and continue the dialogue at a new level (...). It demands an openness toward the world, [a] recogni[tion] that he is never a complete 'being', but always in the process of becoming (...) in childlike curiosity.
>
> (p. 78)

Despite being a vehicle for conversation, Huebner (1963/1999) was critical of scientific knowledge: "The over-valuing of scientific language has led to an undervaluing of religious and aesthetic language" (p. 87). Like many other curricularists who would proceed him, he raised questions about scientific knowledge's predictability and control which transformed, according to Huebner, the "subject-subject" mode of conversation into an "object-subject" one, a milieu where alterity would become "potentially predictable and controllable" (p. 88):

> Today, the prevailing mode of thought would seem to be the subject-object mode, whereby man's basic attitude toward the world of nature and the world of people is that it is something to be known, to be used. The language which speaks of love, of living with, of communion, whether it be uttered by the poet or theologian has its own tiny compartment in man's explanatory and shaping mythologies and does not seep readily into the main currents of man's habits and values.
>
> (p. 89)

Drawing on such criticisms, Huebner unfolded his understanding of love as part of the theological and spiritual con(texts) in the following decade. However, before Huebner had reached such understanding, other curricularists started to give attention to "love" as a basis for curriculum, too. In 1969, Clarence A. Lack wrote an article in *Educational Leadership* posing the question: "*What can be done with love in the redeveloped curriculum?*" (Lack, 1969, p. 693). Arguing that love was germane to "the learning that takes place to fulfill human needs" (Lack, 1969, p. 693), love constituted a "basic part of humanness" (Lack, 1969, p. 394) and satisfied the human need to feel secure. Citing scholars such as Eric Fromm and Carl Jung, Lack (1969) crafted a confounding hodgepodge of ideas around love as the foci for curriculum and learning: holding, motivating, connecting, fulfilling individuals' capabilities, and organizing behaviour, etc. (Lack, 1969).

At that time in the course *of* development, love had seemingly become a vogue for educational theorists and practitioners. In a series of articles published in *Theory into Practice* (henceforth TiP) in 1969, a group of scholars deliberated on the meanings and roles of love, some positioning it as "the highest act of humanity" (Dyer, 1969, p. 104). In "Love is what is," Charles M. Galloway (1969) argued that human's greatest longing is "to be the object of love and to be able to give love" (p 114). Love begins in the "self," its origins "lives within [humans] and that is where [they] can find it. To teach others is to share one's inner strength and beauty" (p. 114). Describing a classroom where a teacher dictated commands and provided callous feedback to students rather than genuinely caring for them, Galloway (1969) claimed that such behaviour could eclipse love in the classroom (including a real love for learning). Drawing from this description on love, he affirmed the paradoxical nature of schooling: "schools are like that. They make you and they break you. They love you and they hate you" (Galloway, 1969, p. 115). Like Lack (1969), Galloway (1969) emphasized the role of love for safety and protection.

Protection is relevant to matters pertaining to love, also writes William F. Pilder. In "Youth: Society's hope for love," Pilder (1969) claimed that the challenge confronting educators concerned the provision of "opportunit[ies] to grow in love [,] to create the possibility for youth to develop a true personal solitude" (p. 119). Like Huebner (1963/1999), Pilder (1969) established a relationship between love and solitude. According to the later, in solitude people would be able to "search for their own beliefs in order to create their definitions" (p. 120). Solitude, Pilder (1969) argued, "can expand the riches of self-knowledge and self-discovery" (p. 120). To love others is to protect such solitude, to border it for intimacy so that "the young can begin to struggle with the problem of self in society" (Pilder, 1969, p. 121), and, ultimately, salute alterity's solitude too (Pilder, 1969).

In addition to protection, "hate" also intersects conversations about love. In "Teaching the Young to Love," Frymier (1969) argued that humans needed to "find a way to learn to live together" (p. 376). "Subject matter, disciplines, and rationality [were] not enough" (p. 377), he decried, adding that unloving behaviour could grow unchecked, from hate to avoidance to discrimination and physical attack, ultimately leading to execution (Frymier, 1969, p. 377). Conversely, speaking out in favour, seeking out people, being altruistic, exerting positive loving behaviours such as touching and caressing, and, lastly, creating life—which he considered the "epitome of loving behavior" (Frymier, 1969, p. 377)—fulfilled the other half of human potential (Frymier, 1969). At schools, educators were called upon to become mindful of their biases (e.g., bias against girls) and foster "positive, creative, and responsive" (Frymier, 1969, p. 378) strategies to help young people become more loving.

Although some curricularists considered hate the opposite of love, there were others who questioned such a dichotomous view. For example, Berman (1969) claimed that the opposite of love was, in fact, "calculative thinking" (p. 97) because "love is concerned with understanding" (p. 97), a phenomenon observed in the process of "truly caring" (p. 97). Although holding some prejudiced assumptions, Berman (1969) maintained that teaching love as a co-response was paramount to children, and, so, she begged the question: "*What can the school do?*" (p. 99). In all these TiP essays, the position of schools as beacons of love was severely questioned. The school and the curriculum (the curriculum-as-plan, the curriculum-as-lived, and especially the hidden curriculum) often constrained love. Yet, as the authors of these articles attested, work towards "love" was possible.

In a fifth essay published in TiP, Prudence Dyer (1969) attested that love *could* be represented and taught via the curriculum as in "love for self, for a mate, for a family, for a fellow man, for a society, for a nation, for ideals, [and] for God" (Dyer, 1969, p. 104). According to Dyer (1969), the natural sciences employed the concept to describe "magnetic attraction and reputation in the language of passions" (p. 104), whereas the social sciences applied it to describe "the role of the family" and "the functions of community helpers who care for them" (p. 104). In order to promote these kinds of "loves" in the curriculum, Dyer (1969) shared examples from the literature regarding each relationship described above. S/he contended:

> Teaching children to love is the ideal—a *possible* dream—if we as teachers first love children—and if we can ourselves be exemplars, knowing and respecting and loving them to an understanding of

the extent and the power of love. Teaching children to love is possible if we can provide an appropriate atmosphere and a curriculum through which mutual love and respect can flourish.

(Dyer, 1969, p. 107)

While some curricularists in the global-north espoused "love" in curriculum by: (i) alluding to a dichotomous world of hate and love; (ii) assigning functional roles to love such as safety and security; and (iii) associating it to kindness, altruism, and conversation, other educators in the global south unfolded another conceptualization of love. One of the most prominent figures to unfold a new conceptualization, the Brazilian pedagogue Paulo Freire, situated love within a standpoint of struggle and liberation, forging a curriculum whose goal was "the radical democratization of schools" (Giroux et al., 2016, p. xi). In his seminal work *Pedagogia do Oprimido* (*Pedagogy of the Oppressed*), Freire deliberated about *conscientização crítica* (English: critical consciousness) while qualifying love, generosity, and solidarity as true or false acts (Portuguese: *"o falso amor,"*[1] *"a generosidade verdadeira," "a solidariedade verdadeira"*) depending on whether individuals involved in the *luta* (English: fight/struggle) fought alongside the oppressed to change their objective reality (Freire, 1970, p. 49). Indeed, Freire (1970) would qualify the struggle for liberation as an "act of love" (p. 45) toward regaining our collective humanity.

When Freire (1970) underscored the oppressive nature of social structures and shed light on the inherent struggles experienced by the oppressed, other curricularists dedicated their work to counteract war, which some perceived as an "inevitable" (Kramp, 1971, p. 1) social event. In 1971, a student from Chapman College wrote a thesis titled "A suggested curriculum to teach love in the elementary school: a system approach." In his thesis, Kramp (1971) affirmed that we "live in an age of weapons" (p. 3) where schools' formal, lived, and hidden curricula often promulgate hate. Citing all the aforementioned articles published in TiP, Kramp (1971) maintained that humans needed to "learn to live together in a peaceful, loving, [and] accepting way" (p. 5). Already imbibing psychological propositions and methods, Kramp (1971) positioned "love" as a construct, a behavioural phenomenon contrived of five variables which needed to be nurtured through the curriculum, including, for instance, positive intersections with peoples. From social struggles to war, the way individuals went about "loving" seemingly differed. Paradoxically, love could lead people to join a struggle to regain their humanity and, at the same time, promote peace and terminate war.

By the 1980's, Huebner continued to dedicate his work to love, but this time focusing on the "transcendent." He underscored that relationships involved "struggle, conflict, forgiveness, love" (Huebner, 1985/1999, p. 344). In his study of the theological con(text), he argued that when individuals experienced the spiritual, one showed "openness and receptivity" (Huebner, 1985/1999, p. 345), a state of vulnerability accompanied by hope, patience, forbearance, sensitivity, and love. According to Huebner (1985/1999), people could experience transcendence in several moments, including when they are "loved and cared for by someone" (p. 346). Studying these transcendent moments, he argued, a pattern of "availability, openness, and vulnerability" (Huebner, 1985/1999, p. 346) to the internal and external world are identified. Keeping oneself available, open, and vulnerable allows for transformations and experiences with the transcendent. Although Huebner (1985/1999) argued that modes of knowing the spiritual do not exist, he claimed:

> Every mode of knowing is also a mode of being in relationship of mutual care and love—often distorted into mere attentiveness and sometimes distorted intro control and oppression—(...) and a mode of waiting, of hope, (...) [and] co-creation.
>
> (pp. 349–350)

"Openness, love, and hope"—the nexus which constituted "the story of human life" (Huebner, 1985/1999, p. 350)—was paramount to new creations, stated Huebner (1985/1999). By distinguishing human love manifested "through care" (Huebner, 1985/1999, p. 374) to God's forgiving and healing love, Huebner (1987/1999) described a "love" that could be improved upon, whose power could support one's reformulation in the world.

Indeed, "love" and "subject reconstruction" seemed to be intertwined, and so was "love" and "education": the process of "leading out from which I am (...) toward that which I am not" (Huebner, 1985/1999, p. 361). In one of his final essays referencing love, he asked: *"What does love do in education?"* (Huebner, 1985/1999, p. 364). Recognizing that the threat of the lure of education requires an acknowledgement of "the possibility that the stranger or alien will overpower us rather than empower us" (Huebner, 1985/1999, p. 363), the only assurance that life will be enhanced rather than destroyed, that such a threat will not undermine us all, is love: love in the form of "care" and "healing" which culminate in "reconciliation" (Huebner, 1985/1999, pp. 363–365). However, although love and reconciliation constituted a lexis for curriculum in Huebner's reconceptualization, as well as cardinal themes to many other curricularists' understandings, the extent to which such subjects remained "alive" in curriculum con(texts) would be contested.

In *Understanding curriculum: An introduction to the study of historical and contemporary curriculum discourses*, Pinar et al. (1995) compiled a series of articles to understand curriculum in its various con(texts): historical, political, racial, gendered, phenomenological, poststructural, (auto)biographical, aesthetic, theological, institutional, and international. Deliberations on love (as a cause, process, and goal of/for education) were mostly absent in these con(texts), emerging less timidly, however, in the phenomenological, theological, and institutionalized understandings of curriculum.

In the theological con(text), alluding to the hidden curriculum, Pinar et al. (1995) claimed that those who could not understand lived experience needed curriculum research to "restore vision and bring knowledge to the innocent in order that they might love" (p. 420). Curriculum as lived was paramount to "educational love, a notion which incorporates patience, hope, serenity, humor, and goodness" (p. 433). In the theological con(text), Pinar et al. (1995) cited a quote where Nel Noddings challenged the idea that humans "enter into the ethical world through fear and not through love" (Nel Noddings in Pinar et al., 1995, p. 657). Speaking through a feminist lens, Noddings claimed that love can inspire ethical thinking: "the desire to be a loving parent is a powerful impetus toward ethical life, and so is the desire to remain in loving relation" (Noddings in Pinar et al., 1995, p. 657). Nodding's work also informed the contour of the institutional con(text) where her curriculum design, inspired on the concept of care, unfolded.

From Bobbitt to Noddings, conceptualizations of "love" had always constituted a lexis for curriculum, but, as already stated, conversations around "love" as sources, means, and/or ends of/for liberation, peace, and/or reconciliation etc. were quite absent in education and society (as indicated in bell hooks' and Jack Miller's autobiographical deliberations, a clear grievance of educationalists). Moreover, as hooks (2000) decried, conversations around "love" had usually been led by men through an understanding of "fantasy" (p. xxiii). However, albeit in absence, love would still emerge, decrying its own existence, pronounced in the work of curricularists/educationalists such as Susan Huddleston Edgerton (1996), hooks (2000), and Schubert (2010), as well as in "internationalist" accounts of curriculum.

Recognizing challenges to promote communication across differences while espousing multicultural approaches to education, Edgerton

(1996) focused on the notion of translation without "a master" (p. 58), which, for her, could not be dissociated from love, that is, power: "love is also about power that is dynamic rather than static and asymmetrical" (p. 9). Bringing the canonical question to evidence (*What knowledge is of most worth?*), Edgerton (1996) suggested a new approach to minimize violence: "*What knowledge best enables us to care for ourselves, one another, and the nonhuman world?*" (pp. 9–10). Speaking of a nexus of "rage, love, and hope" (p. 10), Edgerton (1996) understood that *the course* (re)produced personal and social marginality through encounters (p. 46), and that the definition of margins often crystalizes a "language of opposition" (p. 41).

According to Edgerton (1996), the deconstruction, dialect, and translation that occur in classrooms require "judgement" that cannot come from a place other than love; otherwise it risks "terrorism" (p. 62). Edgerton (1996) emphasized the role of listening and feminist theological interpretations of *agape* and *eros*, one which does not "hierarchicalize" (p. 64) elements such as the spiritual, the sexual, and the romantic: "true love for anyone or anything comes from both mind and body, selflessness, and a kind of selfishness" (p. 66). Such love demands an emotional "investment" without "rejection" (p. 67), that is, a reciprocity, argued Edgerton (1996). Ultimately, Edgerton (1996) employed "love" as an analogy for teaching and learning, one which spurred imagination and disruption, an opening for "translations across differences" (p. 67)—the blurring of boundaries between "self" and "alterity."

Like Edgerton (1996), hooks (2000) spoke of love from a feminist standpoint and underscored the experience of trauma. In her autobiographical account, hooks (2000) claimed that she desired to return in time to experience love once again, but she realized: "We can never go back. I know that now. We can go forward" (p. x). She had to be "really ready to love or be loved in the present" (p. x). Hooks (2000) praised a "return to love" (p. xi) in moving forward, which requires profound changes in collective thinking and action to actualize a "loving culture" (p. xxiv). For hooks (2000), affection and care are just two of the "ingredients" of love: love involves "care, affection, recognition, respect, commitment, and trust, as well as honest and open communication" (p. 5). In sum, hooks (2000) maintained that "love" constituted spiritual growth and, thus, it could not exist in an ambience of abuse. Although "care" could constitute one's situatedness of becoming, giving care did not mean "we are loving" (hooks, 2000, p. 8): "When we are loving we openly and honestly express care, affections, responsibility, respect, commitment, and trust" (p. 14).

Hooks' deliberations on love would inspire the labor of many educationalists and curricularists in "Post-Reconceptualization." For example, Schubert (2010a) claimed that hooks' scholarship was quite helpful. He positioned "love" as a counter-act to Dewey's "acquisitive society" and its competitive and commodified social relations. Schubert (2010a) qualified love as "the moral equivalent to war" (p. 19). In *Curriculum Studies Handbook: The Next Moment*, Nathan Snaza (2010) elaborated 13 theses regarding the state of curriculum, one of which concerned the position of "love," that is, to live aesthetically, a desire for "ethical intervention" rather than "understanding" (p. 52). Responding to Snaza, the same Schubert (2010b) maintained that love in "ethical commitment" was a neglected curriculum reading:

> What *is* clear is that we need to consider that place of love in curriculum studies, in curriculum theorizing, in pedagogical relationship, in *currere*—something that Snaza reminds us well. While he reminds us that this has been addressed by bell hooks, Susan Edgerton, and a few others, *why has it been neglected by so many curricularists?*
>
> (p. 61; emphasis added)

Speaking of love, Schubert (2010b) called upon curriculum workers to inquire who "loved them into being" (p. 57) without employing a deficit lens. Moreover, Schubert (2010b) acclaimed Snaza's call for "creation" and "wonder" more than "discovery" (p. 61) while asking if we are able to love "greed and imperialism out of the state" (p. 61), espousing "ethical-based love commitment" through a nexus of "careful, imaginative, and aesthetic" readings of the "[con]texts of our lives" (pp. 61–62).

The Post-Reconceptualist maneuver toward internationalization (see, for example, Wang, 2012) and, most recently, the burgeoning interest in indigenous scholarship and "rematriation" (Tuck & Gaztambide-Fernández in Downey, 2022, p. 123) also contemplates the position of love in curriculum work. In con(texts) of the East which lay outside the "Anglo-American nexus" (Smith, 2013, p. 46), love has been a pivotal element of long-established wisdom traditions, including Buddhism and Taoism. In these traditions, "love" is often reverberated alongside "receptivity" and "compassion," a lexis of being together in non-violent co-existence in the world. For example, in *Cross-Cultural Studies in Curriculum: Eastern Thought, Educational Insights*, Robert Hattam writes about the Buddhist tradition and the Dalai Lama's theory of social engagement and responsibility (*bodhiccita*): "For

Buddhists, love and compassion, or concern for the welfare of others, are not feelings but types of awareness, (...) a quality of mind" (Hattam, 2008, p. 116). The other side of love is compassion itself: "the wish that others are free from their suffering" (Hattam, 2008, p. 116). Hattam (2008) writes about Buddhists' concern for others, but stresses that, in this tradition, the primary focus is healing the "self" in order to transform mind/heart and serve alterity. "Universal responsibility" (Hattam, 2008, p. 119), the practice of compassion, counteracts a nexus of "greed, envy, and aggressive competitiveness" (p. 119) in the world. Most recently, "love" has also become one of the key elements of "meditative inquiry" in curriculum studies (Kumar, 2013), as well as a topic to be explored in syllabus as curriculum (Rocha, 2022).

Through indigenous scholarship, "love" has been questioned and theorized. For example, in *Curriculum Studies in Canada* (aka CSinC) (2022) (https://curriculumstudiesincanada.com), the work of Hodgson-Smith has been emphasized. She speaks of love in teaching and differentiates the search for knowledge between the "external source" (science) from the "internal nature of knowing" which she qualifies as "love" (Curriculum Studies in Canada, 2022, p. 2). The relationship between teacher and students is underscored, but, like hooks (2000), she is critical of "care" because she perceives it as an "acceptable compromise" (p. 2). Likewise, Rachel Flowers (2015) contests "love" as a mis-recognized "mode of solidarity" (p. 32) with settler society. For Flowers (2015), "love" can deny the validity of "sadness, resentment, and anger" (p. 32) and their transformative potential; love cannot erase anger and rage, as well as the possibility of a "refusal to forgive" (Flowers, 2015, p. 32). Flowers (2015) claims that, for indigenous peoples, *sharing* and *co-existence/co-resistance* are paramount to governance because they underscore interrelatedness towards a "constellation of responsibilities" (p. 35) that halt exploitation, domination, and suffering.

Clearly, for many theoreticians, care is *not* tantamount to love. Love is a much larger concept and cannot be subsumed within a single lexis of "caring"—whether it translates as a responsibility for others and for the world, or a type of awareness, a state of mind; or, alternatively, as a sentiment, a commitment toward others' wellbeing, etc. Moreover, although "love is [often] identified with a resignation of power, and power with a denial of love" (Keith, 2010, p. 2010), many curricularists contend that love can*not* be disassociated from power. For example, Keith (2010) claims that love without power and human connection is "sentimental" and "anaemic," often practiced through a pedagogy of "cordial relations" (p. 540). In this course, we have theorized "love," adding different meanings and practices to it, creating intersections to speak about a myriad of causes, means, and ends of love in and for education. In all accounts, however, care permeates lexis and praxis, whether or not it is masqueraded, intersected, or supplemented by other elements such as "power" and "compassion." When we nurture a love for learning, a love for a place, for the self, for other people and nature, among many other "subjects" and "objects," or when we love to promote liberation or reconciliation, we exert or attempt to exert "care," albeit in different capacities and fashions, as I shall explain and explore in future chapters.

I theorize love in the course *of* development, however. Like Bobbitt (1918), I look into the past in order to foresee possibilities in the future, and to understand the present, but, as I explained in CWSJL, I do so by *running the course* of development, which required the forging and fortification of a nexus of love, hospitality, and solidarity. Indeed, running the course *of* development rather than making comparisons between societies is what have allowed the theorization of love as an ethics of care giving. In *The Curriculum*, Bobbitt (1918) *compared* two kinds of societies and citizens—the small, "primitive" society, and the "modern" one. In his seminal work, Bobbitt (1918) rightly underscored that societies "evolved" and "expanded," thus creating hostilities with neighbouring "tribes." Like Huebner (1999), Bobbitt (1918) highlighted the importance of "existence," albeit with an emphasis on the continuation of one's "tribe" (p. 118) in the course *of* development.

Bobbitt (1918) claimed that, in order to survive, groups needed to exert "social solidarity" (what we call inter-group solidarity today), virtues, and cohesion to outperform other tribes and secure their existence. Consequently, two standards of conduct emerged, one toward fellow citizens and another toward "aliens." The "good citizen" would employ these standards according to the position enjoyed by "alterity." In "contemporary" inter/national affairs, Bobbitt (1918) posited that "inner solidarity" is still needed, and that nation-states have institutionalized their "anti-social tendencies [by] develop[ing] law, traditions, public opinion, [and] military technique" (p. 121). Bobbitt (1918) also posited that we dwell in a paradoxical state wherein institutions operate to promote the welfare of individuals (systematic state care) within the nation-state and, if necessary, the destruction of alien groups, too.

Solidarity is a key element in Bobbitt's conceptualization of "primitive" and "modern" affairs, and also an element of "nexus" in CWSJL where love, the ethics of care, is genesis, a place of caring creation. When we *collectively* run from a fortified nexus of love—a standpoint where we are invited to "return to love" (hooks, 2000, p. xi)—in the very course *of* development, we aspire to go to a place where no structures and power shape and dictate the unfolding of our human and non-human relations; we are called upon to care for and about the dignity, wellbeing, and flourishing of all, being open to give and receive *from within*, that is, to exert genuine hospitality, followed by solidarity. Hence, love as genesis does not espouse the bare minimum, such as existence, but rather *collective thriving* grounded on mutual, symbiotic, relational care.

However, as it is, we live in a hierarchical world whose competitive course and power constrain our experiences with love. Du Bois and Marable (2004) once suggested that people of color "still [had] to seek the freedom of life and limb, the freedom to work and think, the freedom to love and aspire" (p. 6). Dubois was certainly right: those who have holden and accumulated power in the course of development have certainly enjoyed more freedoms to exert and experience care, but I argue that such care is still transfigured by such power and structures, often transgressing itself into forms of control. Indeed, the genuine care which we *could* experience is constrained by power, privilege, oppression, and, consequently, trauma. Paradoxically, love is operationalized *and* constrained by power in a *hierarchical* world of becomings. Not surprisingly, care is usually contested as a lexis and praxis of love, as a nexus for mutual becoming. Yet, I contend that, even in hierarchical ambiences where one may have experienced abuse of some sort, it is possible to return to a regressive *moment* in one's autobiography and see love in the past by analyzing one's life relationally and contextually through "critical bifocality" (Weis & Fine, 2012). I argue that even in smallest glimpses and in transfigured shape, the presence of love can circulate the myriad of circuits of privilege and power, that is, the structures that individuals cannot often transgress (See, for example, Flores & Alfaro, 2022).

A bifocalized regression allows for the study of lives in con(texts)—of one's own and alterity's—to understand how hierarchies and circuits shape our individual *and* collective becoming. A bifocal understanding of "self" and alterity may support less judgmental thinking. Moreover, a bifocal lens may support an understanding of how "care" circulates these structures, often hidden under cloaks of control. A bifocalized regression can allow for a more loving progression, an attempt to return to love in the future which is the present: we find "love" in the past so that it becomes more tangible in our unfolding, in our subject reconstruction, and in nurturing future relations of care—a progressive moment where power becomes less prevalent, where love is no longer negotiated, but only proliferated. Of course, this is no simple labor because hierarchies are needed to maintain the tripod of our *current* development: order, security, and wellbeing, the latter been added to the list in recent post/modern times.

As I shall deliberate in the next chapter, caring for and about in a hierarchical world full of divergencies is a "complicated conversation." But I argue that this should not prevent the labor ahead. While the writing of a single autobiography might not bring our "selves" back to love at once, a commitment to unfolding as a journey towards love and justice might bring our whole collective closer to more loving becoming(s) in the course *of* development, in education (and beyond). This is *the* study that I offer in the next chapters.

Note

1 As indicated by Samuel D. Rocha (2022), the translation of *Pedagogy of the Oppressed* (Freire, 1970) is commendable and yet reductive. Several terms from the original Portuguese version (Freire, 1968) are not included in the English translation, including, but not limited to, the term "falso amor" (English: false love), encountered in the Portuguese version, chapter 1.

References

Apple, M. W. (2018). Critical curriculum studies and the concrete problems of curriculum policy and practice. *Journal of Curriculum Studies*, *50*(6), 685–690. https://doi.org/10.1080/00220272.2018.1537373

Aoki, T. (2005). Teaching as in-dwelling between two curriculum worlds. In W. F. Pinar & R. L. Irwin (Eds.), *Curriculum in a new key: The collected works of Ted T. Aoki* (pp. 159–166). Essay, Lawrence Erlbaum Associates.

Baker, J. K., Cousins, S., & Johnston-Wilder, S. (2019). Mathematics: A place of loving kindness and resilience-building. *Journal of the Canadian Association for Curriculum Studies*, *17*(1), 111–126.

Berman, L. M. (1969). Teaching love as co-response. *Theory into Practice*, *8*(2), 96–100. https://doi.org/10.1080/00405846909542181

Bobbitt, J. F. (1909). Practical eugenics. *The Pedagogical Seminary*, *16*(3), 385–394. https://doi.org/10.1080/08919402.1909.10532596

Bobbitt, J. F. (1912). The elimination of waste in education. *The Elementary School Teacher*, *12*(6), 259–271. https://doi.org/10.1086/454122

Bobbitt, J. F. (1918). *The curriculum*. Houghton.

Cambridge Dictionary. (2008). Juxtapose. In *Cambridge advanced learner's dictionary* (3rd ed.). Cambridge University Press.

Curriculum Studies in Canada. (2022). Aboriginal learning styles and pedagogy. CSinC. http://curriculumstudiesincanada.ca/research-briefs/

Deng, Z. (2018). Contemporary curriculum theorizing: Crisis and resolution. *Journal of Curriculum Studies, 50*(6), 691–710. https://doi.org/10.1080/0022 0272.2018.1537376

Downey, A. M. (2022). (Re)membering indigenous curriculum theorists: Gifts and gratitude. In C. Shields, A. G. Podolski, & J. J. G. Yallop (Eds.), *Influences and inspirations in curriculum studies research and teaching reflections on the origins and legacy of contemporary scholarship* (pp. 123–129). Routledge.

Du Bois, W. E. B., & Marable, M. (2004). *Souls of black folk* (1st ed.). Routledge. https://doi.org/10.4324/9781315631998

Dyer, P. (1969). Love in curriculum. *Theory Into Practice, 8*(2), 104–107. https://doi.org/10.1080/00405846909542183

Edgerton, S. H. (1996). *Translating the curriculum: Multiculturalism into cultural studies*. Routledge.

Egan, K. (2003). What is curriculum? *Journal of the Canadian Association for Curriculum Studies, 1*(1), 9–16. Retrieved August 6, 2022, from https://jcacs.journals.yorku.ca/index.php/jcacs/issue/view/711

Flores, J., & Alfaro, A. R. (2022). Critical pedagogy: Loving and caring within and beyond the classroom. *Curriculum Inquiry, 52*(3), 385–396. https://doi.org/10.1080/03626784.2022.2072665

Flowers, R. (2015). Refusal to forgive: Indigenous women's love and rage. *Decolonization: Indigeneity, Education & Society, 4*(2), 32–49.

Frymier, J. R. (1969). Teaching the young to love. *Theory into Practice, 8*(2), 42–47. https://doi.org/10.1080/00405846909542170

Galloway, C. M. (1969). Love is what it is. *Theory into Practice, 8*(2), 114–116. https://doi.org/10.1080/00405846909542186

Gaztambide-Fernández, R. A. (2009). Representing curriculum. *Curriculum Inquiry, 39*(1), 235–253. https://doi.org/10.1111/j.1467-873x.2008.01448.x

Giroux, H., Gourani, P., Macedo, D., & Grollios, G. (2016). Foreword. In N. Gakoudi (Trans.), *Paulo Freire and the Curriculum* (pp. vii–xx). Routledge.

Gleibermann, E. (2016). A curriculum of love. *Tikkun, 31*(4), 54–57. https://doi.org/10.1215/08879982-3676912

Greene, M. (1995). *Releasing the imagination: Essays on education, the arts, and social change*. Jossey-Bass Publishers.

Grumet, M., Anderson, A., & Osmond, C. (2008). Finding form for curriculum research. In K. Gallagher (Ed.), *The methodological dilemma: Creative, critical and collaborative approaches to qualitative research* (pp. 136–156). Routledge.

Hattam, R. (2008). Socially-engaged buddhism as a provocation for critical pedagogy in unsettling times. In *Cross-cultural studies in curriculum: Eastern thought, educational insights* (pp. 109–136). Routledge.

hooks, b. (2000). *All about love: New visions*. Harper Perennial.

hooks, b. (2018). *All about love: New visions*. William Morrow, an imprint of HarperCollins Publishers.

Huebner, D. E. (1962a/1999). Classroom action. In K. F. Hillis & W. Pinar (Eds.), *The lure of the transcendent: Collected essays by Dwayne E. Huebner* (pp. 66–73). Essay, Routledge.

Huebner, D. E. (1962b/1999). Is the elementary curriculum adequate? In K. F. Hillis & W. Pinar (Eds.), *The lure of the transcendent: Collected essays by Dwayne E. Huebner* (pp. 10–14). Essay, Routledge.

Huebner, D. E. (1962c/1999). Knowledge and the curriculum. In K. F. Hillis & W. Pinar (Eds.), *The lure of the transcendent: Collected essays by Dwayne E. Huebner* (pp. 44–65). Essay, Routledge.

Huebner, D. E. (1963/1999). New modes of man's relationship to man. In K. F. Hillis & W. Pinar (Eds.), *The lure of the transcendent: Collected essays by Dwayne E. Huebner* (pp. 74–93). Essay, Routledge.

Huebner, D. E. (1985/1999). Spirituality and knowing. In K. F. Hillis & W. Pinar (Eds.), *The lure of the transcendent: Collected essays by Dwayne E. Huebner* (pp. 340–352). Essay, Routledge.

Huebner, D. E. (1999). In V. Hillis & W. F. Pinar (Eds.), *The lure of the transcendent: Collected essays by Dwayne E. Huebner*. Lawrence Erlbaum Associates. https://doi.org/10.4324/9780203053706

Jales Coutinho, A. M. (2022). *Curriculum work and social justice leadership in a post-reconceptualist era: Attaining critical consciousness and learning to become* (1st ed.). Routledge. https://doi.org/10.4324/9781003188629

Jung, J. (2016). *The concept of care in curriculum studies: Juxtaposing Currere and Hakbeolism*. Routledge.

Jung, J.-H., & Pinar, W. F. (2016). Conceptions of curriculum. *The SAGE Handbook of Curriculum, Pedagogy and Assessment: Two Volume Set, 1*, 29–46. https://doi.org/10.4135/9781473921405.n2

Keith, N. (2010). Getting beyond anaemic love: From the pedagogy of cordial relations to a pedagogy for difference. *Journal of Curriculum Studies, 42*(4), 539–572. https://doi.org/10.1080/00220270903296518

Kramp, D. (1971). *A suggested curriculum to teach love in the elementary school: A systems approach* (dissertation). Chapman University.

Kumar, A. (2013). *Curriculum as meditative inquiry*. Palgrave Macmillan.

Lack, C. A. (1969). Love as a basis for organizing curriculum. *Educational Leadership, 26*(7), 693.

Malewski, E. (2010). *Curriculum studies handbook: the next moment*. Routledge.

Mason, M. M., & Mason, M. M. (1929). Suggestions towards a curriculum part III—The love of knowledge. In *School education volume III* (pp. 240–247). Routledge.

Miller, J. E. (2005). *The sound of silence breaking: Women, autobiography, curriculum*. Peter Lang.

Miller, J. P. (2018). *Love and compassion: Exploring their role in education*. University of Toronto Press.

Moore, A. (2015). *Understanding the school curriculum: Theory, politics and principles*. Routledge.

Morgan-Klein, B., & Osborne, M. (2007). *The concepts and practices of lifelong learning* (1st ed.). Routledge. https://doi.org/10.4324/9780203932766

Pilder, W. F. (1969). Youth: Society's hope for love. *Theory into Practice, 8*(2), 119–121. https://doi.org/10.1080/00405846909542188

Pinar, W. F. (1999). Introduction. In V. Hillis (Ed.), *The lure of the transcendent: Collected essays by Dwayne E. Huebner* (pp. XV–XXVIII). Lawrence Erlbaum Associates.

Pinar, W. F. (2006). *The synoptic text today and other essays curriculum development after the reconceptualization*. Peter Lang.

Pinar, W. F. (2007). *Intellectual advancement through disciplinarity: Verticality and horizontality in curriculum*. Sense.

Pinar, W. F. (2008). Curriculum theory since 1950: Crisis, reconceptualization, internationalization. In F. M. Connelly, M. F. He, & J. Phillion (Eds.), *The SAGE handbook of curriculum and instruction* (pp. 491–513). Sage.

Pinar, W. F. (2009). *The worldliness of a cosmopolitan education: Passionate lives in public service*. Routledge.

Pinar, W. F. (2011). *The character of curriculum studies: Bildung, currere, and the recurring question of the subject*. Palgrave Macmillan.

Pinar, W. F. (2016). Working from within, together. In M. A. Doll (Ed.), *The reconceptualization of curriculum studies* (pp. 194–205). Routledge.

Pinar, W. F., Reynolds, W. M., Slattery, P., & Taubman, P. M. (1995). *Understanding curriculum: An introduction to the study of historical and contemporary curriculum discourses*. Peter Lang.

Rocha, S. (2022). *Syllabus as curriculum: A reconceptualist approach*. Routledge.

Schubert, W. H. (2010a). Language, legacy, and love in curriculum. In B. S. Stern & D. J. Flinders (Eds.), *Curriculum and teaching dialogue* (Vol. 12, pp. 1–23). IAP.

Schubert, W. H. (2010b). Response to Nathan Snaza: Love in ethical commitment: A neglected curriculum reading. In E. Malewski (Ed.), *Curriculum studies handbook: The next moment* (pp. 57–62). Routledge.

Smith, D. G. (2013). Wisdom responses to globalization. In W. F. Pinar (Ed.), *International handbook of curriculum research* (2nd ed., pp. 45–49). Essay, Routledge.

Snaza, N. (2010). Thirteen theses on the question of state in curriculum studies. In E. Malewski (Ed.), *Curriculum studies handbook: The next moment* (pp. 43–56). Routledge.

Strong-Wilson, T. (2021). *Teachers' ethical self-encounters with counter-stories in the classroom: From implicated to concerned subjects*. Routledge, Taylor & Francis Group.

Valencia, R. R. (2020). *International deficit thinking: Educational thought and practice*. Routledge.

Wals, A., Pinar, W., & Macintyre, T. (2022). Curriculum and pedagogy in a changing world. In E. A. Vickers, K. Pugh, & L. Gupta (Eds.), *Education and context in reimagining education: The international science and evidence based education assessment* [A. K. Duraiappah, N. V. van Atteveldt et al. (eds.)]. UNESCO MGIEP. In Press.

Wang, H. (2012). A nonviolent perspective on internationalizing curriculum studies. In W. F. Pinar (Ed.), *International handbook of curriculum research* (2nd ed., pp. 67–76). Routledge.

Weis, L., & Fine, M. (2012). Critical bifocality and circuits of privilege: Expanding critical ethnographic theory and design. *Harvard Educational Review,82*(2),173–201.https://doi.org/10.17763/haer.82.2.v1jx34n441532242

3 Positioning love as an ethics of care/giving in curriculum

Love as an ethics of care/giving has permeated the fabric of my complicated conversations, but, as I have alluded to in CWSJL, I doubt here and then that the meaning of love has been proliferated in my life—*Does love truly exist?*

At times, I feel that the way I go about loving in my daily encounters is a negotiating act (too many human and non-human actors involved and affected by a myriad of decisions, too many hypotheses and lack of prior knowledge, etc.) rather than an evolving act of love-as-genesis—*Can we love every relational encounter as if trust has been already built and never been eroded? Can we love as if our actions would not ultimately harm any being in the planet, but rather constitute a part of a symbiotic, ritually evolving, and dialectical act of giving and receiving care? Ultimately, can we love to make all suffering and vulnerability in the world a myth, just like meritocracy, by enacting a symbiotic act of (just) giving in the course of development?*

As a seeker, I am now inclined to run this course questioning everything that constitutes my surroundings, and also my own thoughts. One may think that this kind of "critical thinking" is just what one aspires to achieve in life and at work. Or perhaps that this is the kind of thought that may drag one to a continuous spiral loop, bringing the "self" to dubiousness. The truth is: What a difficult labor this is, especially when one continuously questions the very basis from which one can relate (see "Fortifying nexus" in CWSJL) by forging hypotheses capable of dismantling love from within. More often than not, I would say that such labor can cause more levels of suffering than liberation— liberation from the very structures we attempt to transgress; liberation from the knowledge we mobilize and which can become a venue for single thoughts, too; and liberation to love when structures and dogmas can command dispositions that purposefully unleash acts of single and collective harm.

DOI: 10.4324/9781003359968-3

These questions have brought my "self" to this current moment, to pose a leading, puzzling query for curricularists labouring in the intersections of theory, policy, and practice: *Can we become liberated from the discourses and con(texts) that make up the constraining fabrics of this world in order to proliferate rather than negotiate love in our daily encounters with self, alterity, nature, and the cosmos?*

I write this text thinking of love and of my own autobiographical encounters in the world to inspire new becomings. After all, we are all unfolding as we engage in this complicated and yet necessary conversation. Although questioning the meaning of love may position people farther away from its nexus, such questioning is pivotal, too, because we live within hierarchies. Here, I argue that while seeking to fortify love in our lives, we have to critically study the care that permeates the hierarchies in order to not fall prey to masquerading discourses and practices (the unsentimental hospitality) which *de facto* serve to sustain and proliferate power. By studying love, we might be able to identify glimpses of love within hierarchies in regression *and* imagine what true, genuine care may be/feel like too (in a world where people do not have to negotiate it due to power dynamics culminating from hierarchical arrangements) so as to attempt to proliferate it in our synthesis, finding ways to actualize the course otherwise. I contend that the critical study and the fortification of love constitute another paradoxical element of post-reconceptualization, this transitory and ever-lasting state between "the paradoxical" and what some would consider "the ideal."

Experiencing collective care would be the ideal world to live in. But, unfortunately, we still have to remain critical (or, I would say, vigilant) of the care we experience in our current state of being and becoming because not everybody is willing *to give* in the course, and for justifiable reasons.... First, many people have difficulties experiencing and visualizing the love that permeates their lives due to structures and oppression. I speak of individuals who may feel neglected and betrayed in/by the course of running, from inception onwards, for one or more reasons. Not surprisingly, these individuals become inclined to act suspiciously without giving trust and love in a dichotomous world of takers *and* givers. Indeed, in a burgeoning state of hierarchical upbringing, conflict, and (collective) trauma, I reckon that our complicated "selves" are often prone to enacting some form of unsentimental hospitality and solidarity while eschewing love.

One might conclude that, in such an upbringing, one is better off by becoming a "taker" than a "giver." I do not write these as demeaning statements, however. As I will soon point out in my autobiographical excerpts, I have once believed that love did not constitute my own situatedness of becoming, for I began to negotiate its meanings during my (inter)actions with alterity whilst attributing hidden meanings of avarice, mistrust, and the like to these human interactions—and so I thank nature, the arts, and a few human interactions for helping me believe that, despite structures, love still permeates our collective circumstance of becoming within the hierarchies.

While criticality is important for the course *of* development, if we question love too much without departing from a nexus of love, we may end up falling prey to deconstructing the very basis from which to relate. In running this course of complicated conversations, readers will notice that I negotiate the meaning of love continuously—and yet I attempt to bring "the whole" of my writing and subjectivities into a nexus, seeking to fortify love, a standpoint where caregiving is celebrated and proliferated in curriculum work (and beyond). I strive to hold on to the meanings of care/giving which have permeated my life as I felt embraced by "the other," nature, and the cosmos while experiencing the power which circulated my con(texts). Despite good levels of criticality, full skepticism should not dominate the shapes and colours of our hearts. After all, no course can be sustained without trust (and love).

Perhaps, as more individuals start to become *consciente* and loving in the world, we may position our humanity to become *less* judgmental of others and only *more* studious and loving of such relationships—an "ongoing ethical engagement with alterity" (Pinar, 2015, p. xi)—, departing from the nexus to love the unfolding brand-new world of becomings. There might be a moment in our regression and progression where criticality must only be sustained for the "self"—as we continue to battle self-aggrandizing absorptivity, bifocalizing "self" and "work" (see CWSJL) to unfold, to run this complicated course of development. While mind (reason) and intuition may call upon our "selves" to act vengefully at times, I contend that humanity should not *dwell* on such feelings in the course *of* development. Rather, we should attempt to *return to love* and, hence, fortify it. The sanguine vision of *nexus* must stand as collective lighthouse, the standpoint that we shall abide to as we build and cross bridges to relate and to forge nexus with our "selves," "alterity," "nature," and the "cosmos."

Listening to Rita L. Irwin refer to Ted Aoki's bridge, which is located in the Nitobe Memorial Garden of the University of British Columbia (UBC) (Irwin, 2022), the image of "in-betweenness" lingers: the bridge connects two space(s) divided and (yet) linked by the same tranquil

Positioning love as an ethics of care/giving in curriculum 37

Image 3.1 Ted Aoki's bridge in UBC's Nitobe Memorial Garden. Photographed by Nicole Lee & Joanne Ursino and here reprinted with their permission.

waters, two shores, and one peaceful view (see Image 3.1). The bridge, the relational, is the love, attempting to create an intersection, a nexus, between the two, opposing sides. This is the difficult labor which awaits our selves: to not only build those bridges, but to sustain, and to cross them, meeting somewhere in the middle before departing to new context(s), continuing the journey, seeking, bifocalizing, facing other bridges, novel kinds of "in-betweenness." The allusion to "the bridge" (Wang, 2013, p. 69) and to "in-betweens" (Wang, 2013, p. 72) trends in internationalization of "peace studies."

This is also the tenderly message that the Nitobe Memorial Garden (NMG) aspires to transmit to visitors: a traditional Japanese stroll garden and tea house, NMG celebrates the memory of Inazô Nitobe (1862–1933), a Japanese intellectual who longed to "promote a better understanding of Japanese culture in the West, [and] to become a bridge across the Pacific" (UBC Botanical Garden, 2021). To study lives, especially our own, relationally and contextually, naming circuits of privilege and oppression and disrupting single thoughts while departing from a fortified nexus of love towards love and justice: This is the post-reconceptualist and internationalist labor of curriculum as a collective public moral enterprise.

Laboring in the Post-Reconceptualist maneuver toward internationalization, we might also linger with the writing of curriculum workers such as Ted Aoki (Aoki et al., 2012) and emerging (international) scholars who bring together "intra and intergenerational conversations" (Malewski, 2010, p. xi) about Aoki's curriculum contributions; scholars who come together to forge "sedimentation [which] will contribute to other sedimentations" (Lee et al., 2022, p. 2)—and, I might add, sedimentations of *and* for love.

Inspired in the 2019 symposium of the Canadian Society for the Study of Education (CSSE), the 2022 edited Routledge volume *Lingering with the Works of Ted T. Aoki: Historical and Contemporary Significance for Curriculum Research and Practice* (henceforth LWTTA) advanced personal and collective understanding(s) of lingering "in tensionality in the in-between" (Lee et al., 2022, p. 3) whilst attending to several relational con(texts), including the temporal and the spatial. LWTTA unveiled several "practices" of 'lingering contemplations,' including that of *caring* (see Lee et al., 2022). Nicole Y. S. Lee, Lesley E. Wong, and Joanne M Ursino rightly remind us in LWTTA that, as we "dwell together humanly" (Ted Aoki in Lee et al., 2022, p. 5) in some form of slow scholarship and labor—meeting in the middle of that bridge, people of all faiths and creeds—, we are invited to stay, to *dwell* individually and collectively. But we are also called upon to depart... in thought and in action, *running* this course of a complicated conversation: two seemingly opposing actions (to dwell and to run), but actions that surely intersect with each other to forge, together with critical bifocality, a nexus for curriculum work.

In facing "the whole" of humanity, dwelling in that bridge, we are invited to experience the new anew: our "selves" and alterity, facing each other, seeking con(texts) to "become subjective and historical" (Pinar, 2011, p. 39), as well as *consciente* with others in subject (re)construction. Bridges can certainly support our collective Post-Reconceptualist labor—I would go as far to contend that they are quite necessary—, but, unfortunately, bridges can also be bound to break. As we are called upon to dwell and to run, we are constantly asked: *which curriculum project do we aspire to actualize? Is it a project where love is fortified, negotiated, deconstructed, negated?* Once again, this book calls upon curricularists to come together to fortify the nexus of love, to return and to proliferate love in regression, progression, analysis, and synthesis—to *give care from within* in increasingly antagonistic, competitive, and divisive times.

So, how could we possibly return to love, to not negotiate it, but rather to proliferate it in the course? Attempting to answer this question, I write about hierarchy, power, capability, and difference, and juxtapose the "theological," "racial," and "aesthetic" discursive con(texts) (Pinar et al., 1995) of this complicated conversation. As indicated in CWSJL, humans started to create structures to promote order and security. Through the creation of structures, communities began to garner power, that is, capabilities to "organize" the difference that they identified and named aiming to promote "order" and "security." In liberal democracy, capabilities are often considered a product of the iteration between intellectual prowess and industriousness, which culminate in material capabilities. Of course, the "aesthetic" can intersect with the "racial" to produce inferior discourses through the "ideational" con(text), which plays a role in selection and streaming, in the organization of difference and in the production of inequalities in geographical con(texts), too (e.g., Monk et al., 2021).

Difference exists regardless of power and structures, but structures and power (capabilities) have organized difference in the course of development. We can name difference in love, and we can name difference in conflict, which is a different type of naming. Naming in conflict is immediate: there is no playful wonder, only dismissive hypothesis and assumptions, leading to questioning at best. In love, wonder proliferates, culminates in conversation. In fact, "wonder might become replaced by sentiments of 'familiarity'" (Salmón, 2000, in Varga & Shear, 2022, p. 10) which are intrinsic to relationality, to love. But wonder can also be transformed and culminate in possessive desire and, ultimately, objectification (see, for example, Varga & Shear, 2022). Unfortunately, we do not dwell in "complicated conversations" in our current course *of* development, but rather in a state of delusion, red tape, surveillance...

In our current state of affairs, we often learn to respect difference in the family, but it might also be in the family that we learn *about* difference firsthand (e.g. motherhood and fatherhood and their different social roles). Learning about difference within and outside the household as young children, we also learn about power. Indeed, family dynamics might constitute the genesis for such understanding, even if not openly discussed by caregivers. Going to school, difference is further restated through competition and ranking. The question might not be how schools ought to teach "respect" or "tolerance" for difference, playing its paradoxical role in the course of development, which Popkewitz (2009) conceived as a "double gesture" (p. 301). The cardinal question might be how to teach love, how to return to love both in regression and progression, despite our differences, and in our own analysis of the world, in order to proliferate love in our synthesis, in our becoming.

Difference will exist in the world no matter what. The question then becomes "*how to teach difference from love?*" If we regress in the course *of* development to a place of genesis, recognizing that humans were not the first to come into existence—either in theological or scientific, evolutionary con(texts)—, we are brought back to land, to the cosmos, to birth and creation. Indigenous peoples are perhaps the communities that have been closer to love in the course *of* development in postmodernity. As such, the question becomes "*How can we teach about difference through/from land and the cosmos?*" As indicated by many indigenous scholars, land and the ecologies of the earth do not teach us about power as capability, but about *care, balance, symbiotic relationships*, and *co-sharing* (see, for example, Eppert, 2021; Osmond-Johnson & Turner, 2020; Styres, 2017). The focus on balance, relationality, and co-sharing (not power as capability, dependency, structures, and competition) in indigenous writings and teachings may be one of the gifts we have in finding our way back to love, to proximity, and to relational restorations in *collective* unfolding, in classrooms (and beyond).

For example, Western societies have learned to appreciate and desire Whiteness and certain types of phenotypes in the course *of* development. While a scholar construct of race would only emerge centuries later, traits such as "exactness" and "whiteness" had already started to be appreciated as "beauty" in the period of "enlightenment" (See Hall, 1996; Haughton, 2004; Painter, 2011). Meanwhile, other drawings became the venue for anthropological work as a study of deviation and otherness in the same course of development (Hartigan, 1997). Some contend that the teaching of curriculum focused on Whiteness as a racial con(text) has become a site of social (re)production in curriculum work (see, for example, Peters, 2015). When we invite or host "the other" as social beings living in hierarchies, we tend to name difference while reading aesthetically based on "textures" that have been imposed on us through culture and media, all of which determine what constitutes "beauty." Of course, critical scholars have already started to unsettle the aesthetic con(text) (see, for example, Kang, 1996). However, by teaching difference *and* aesthetics through land, we might come to appreciate beauty as relationality too, the *joyful energy* we share with one another, the type of energy one exudes when meeting with a lifelong, high-spirited friend and a loved one, or the type of energy one witnesses in other symbiotic natural encounters—the energy that opens up space for genuine hospitality, for vulnerability in receiving and in naming our differences in the collective, symbiotic act of unfolding lives, within and across con(texts).

It is important to note, however, that defining the problem and solution in development is often a contested terrain (see, for example, Andrews, 2014; Jales Coutinho, 2022; Loutzenheiser, 2014; Tuck, 2009). The problem we face is not the aesthetic and racial con(texts) as the (re) production of Whiteness per se. Here, I contend that Whiteness may be the most eminent *reflection* of "the problem" *of* development: the production of hierarchies that enact power and which condition social relations. Although it is important to question and investigate how people have benefited from Whiteness as racial con(text) in the course of development, by focusing our critical lenses solely on this construct, we might miss the opportunity to fully engage with the complexity of "the problem," which involves the inflated human ego, the creation of structures, the erasure of relationalities, and the culmination of the Anthropocene. Of course, Whiteness has rightly become one of the focus points of critical curriculum studies, but again, we should employ "critical bifocality" (Weis & Fine, 2012) to study how multiple discursive and material con(texts) can/have/will produce(d), reproduce(d), contest(ed), and intersect(ed) each other in the course *of* development.

In sum, humankind disrupted balance and relationality in the course *of* development when our ego lured us into believing that we could control land, alterity, and the ecologies of the earth through our knowledge and capability acquisition, through objectification, and, ultimately, through the creation of our social structures—the same structures which paradoxically serve order and security and which jeopardize the wellbeing of marginalized populations. If we speak metaphorically through the theological con(text) and engage in a "re-reading" of Genesis (see, for example, Oscarson, 2019), humankind could be represented as Adam and Eve, the snake as the ego, and the apple as the frontier, the desired object of knowledge. The ego lured humans to take the frontier for themselves, and we followed suit, starting what we call the era of the Anthropocene. The course *of* development as we know it today had then been initiated. From love and genuine hospitality, from the place of harmony and relationality, from genesis, we departed, finding our selves in a constant fight toward forms of solidarity, a place where *negotiation* of care/giving became the *aiding* vernacular of development.

Indeed, *negotiating* care does not only constitute the "situatedness of becoming" of a single person in the course, but of whole collectives. Oliveira (2015) has made visible the hard negotiations that Mexican mothers living in the United States and their families have to do when they care for their children "here and there" (p. 4). Working with and alongside these "constellations of care," Oliveira documented how the lives of these youth and children differ across borders (Oliveira, 2018, 2020). Bruhn & Oliveira (2021) have also explored how women negotiate "daughterhood as part of their carework, transcend[ing] generational roles and identities" (p. 3). In our world of vulnerabilit(ies), "constellations of care" are often divided by the forces of immigration, as people fly their not-so-safe, not-so-comfort zones to look for better living prospects, transcending within and across con(texts) whilst attempting to forge nexuses—for themselves and for their loved ones.

As I attempt to bifocalize and unfold my own autobiographical lexis, I imagine that these mothers and families long to forge proximity whilst fortifying a nexus of love to bridge feelings, sentiments, and actions... to bring their constellations of loving individuals together to genesis, once again—be it "here or there," "now and then"—while attempting to cross mental, temporal, and physical bridges, to name a few. Symbiotic constellations of care/giving—the love-as-genesis that surpass and overflow borders, including national ones—might as well be one of the key facets of our post-reconceptualist labor. Once again, I argue that we (scholars, practitioners, and policymakers) ought to labor to proliferate love in/through our lives and work, departing from its nexus to dwell, to run, and to bifocalize, changing the course *of* development with/through our "subjectivementalities" (see Chapter 4 in Jales Coutinho, 2022, for a definition of subjectivementality) and new becoming(s).

3.1 The way we go about caring: understanding convergences and divergencies

Of course, as already suggested, the meanings which people attribute to "care" are various. Most recently, the curricularist Owis Bishop has conducted a qualitative, art-based interview study with QTBIPOC (Queer, Trans, Black, Indigenous, People of Color) educators laboring on the traditional territories of the Mississaugas of the Credit River, in the province of Ontario, Canada, to unfold a lexis of "queer care" in education, a "futurity" which calls upon educators to "reimagine and disrupt their knowledge of care and care practices that are built upon White, colonial, and cisheteronormative assumptions" (Owis, 2022, p. iii).

Bishop's understanding of care is surely based on intersectionalities, lived experiences, and study. Raised in Canada and acknowledging their status as a settler and QTBIPOC scholar (Queer, Trans, Black, Indigenous, and People of Color), Bishop draws from the contribution of several other scholars—including Piepzna-Samarasinha (2018) and Chatzidakis et al. (2020)—to unfold their theory of a "queer ethics of care," a theory that challenges performative schooling practices. Bishop refers to "expansive, disruptive, and transgressive care" promoted by educators—a type of care which creates "authentic, fluid, mutually vulnerable relationships with students; explicitly anticolonial, antiracist movements in their teaching and interactions with students; and affirmation and recognition as moments of healing" (Owis, 2022, p. 36). Drawing this understanding of care, Bishop also acknowledges that the concepts of "care" employed in the fields of education and psychology are conflicting (Owis, 2022). Bishop is certainly right: it is inevitable that divergencies in meaning(s) and understanding(s) exist as we attempt to proliferate love as part of this "complicated conversation" (Pinar, 2011, p. xv) in a hierarchical world.

Highlighting the intrinsic relationship between the "ethics of care" and "curriculum," Jung-Hoon Jung juxtaposes *currere*—the infinitive form of curriculum (Pinar & Grumet, 1976)—and *Hakbeolismo*—an indigenous Korean concept that conveys social meanings of earned academic prestige—to converse with scholars about contradictory practices and theories in education. Focusing particularly on *Hakbeolism*, Jung espouses the meanings that circulate competitive and comparative educational practices which may be responsible for enduring human losses both within and across Western and non-Western con(texts), including Jung's home country, the Republic of Korea (see Jung, 2016). Through curriculum's infinitive form, Jung (2016) invites a project for self-understanding and for creative relational transformations. In his work, he urges curricularists to "rescue subjectivity" through an ethical project of self-study, one which is concerned with the unfolding of 'authentic relationships' as a form of "self-care" (Jung, 2016, p. 5).

Similar to Owis (2022), Jung (2016) refers to Nel Noddings' ethics of care in his work. As noted in the previous chapter, Noddings is an eminent ethicist and curricularist. In *Contemporary curriculum discourses: 20 years of JCT*, Noddings (1988) explained her evolving theory on care. At that time in her scholarly trajectory, Noddings claimed that there were three types of caring relationships (among humans), each containing three elements, two necessary and one characteristic: engrossment, reception, and external action, respectively.

Noddings (1988) claimed that to care *from within* requires engrossment, a displaced interest of one's own reality towards that of the other. One can look at the objective reality and image it as one's own—which prompts an "immediate feeling to (...) reduce the pain and actualize the dream" (p. 44), to think about a different reality for alterity, a possibility... One takes part in a "physical becoming" (p. 44) when one is only interested in one's pleasure and pain: "whatever s/he sees in others is preselected in relation to his/her own needs and desires, [that is], s/he does not see the reality of the other as a possibility for [the self]" (Noddings, 1988, p. 44).

Noddings (1988) indicated that we usually project our own reality onto others rather than living experiences vicariously, transforming "the other" into an "object of study and manipulation" (p. 45). However, caring is *not* tantamount to objectification, she argued. In transforming what one receives into "a problem"—the type of thinking taught and emulated by policymakers, what some scholars would have named a deficit oriented praxis—"we move away from the other" (p. 45). A caring relationship occurs when one considers "the cared-for's nature, [her] way of life, needs, and desires" (Noddings, 1988, p. 45), thus creating "a tie" (p. 45) (a relation) where one is constantly pulled into communication. In other words, "caring involves stepping out of one's own personal frame of reference into the other's (...). Our attention, our mental engrossment is on the cared-for, not on ourselves" (p. 51). Further, "when we care, we are touched by the other and expect to touch [alterity]. We enter into a relation with the student, but that relation need not be one of interference and control" (p. 51). In other words, when caring, one "receives the other" (Noddings, 1988, p. 45) without having to understand him/her as a precondition. One *gives* and demonstrates a "quality of disposability" (Noddings, 1988, p. 47). At the bottom line, the relationship is considered "nonrational" (p. 48) as if it was not governed by means-and-ends motivations. "The one-caring is engrossed in the other, not in herself. There is a move from egoism" (p. 50). Noddings (1988) speak about a similar and yet different "tripod" when we engage in caring relationships: "welfare, protection, and enhancement" of "the cared-for" (p. 50) (...). That is, "we act not to achieve for ourselves a commendation but to protect and enhance the welfare of the cared-for" (p. 52): the "one-caring desires the wellbeing of the cared-for and acts to promote that wellbeing" (p. 52)

Jung (2016) underscores the aspects that make Noddings' expansive ethics an appealing frame for his scholarship and for curriculum work in general. Initially working alongside curricularists at UBC, Jung

(2016) went through a process of self-awakening where he was able to understand his "breakdown" and "arrest" to reconstruct his "self." In his relational encounters with UBC scholars, he realized that they did not "talk to [him], but rather listened, their focus to help (...) [his] 'grow[th] and *actualiz[ation]*.'" (p. 35). For him, that constituted *care*, support, and respect. *Currere* allowed Jung (2016) to embark on "a journey of care through self-understanding" (p. 44) while Noddings' three roots of ethics (ontology, pragmatism, and the feminine perspective) created the foundation for an understanding of a "care-for-others" (Jung, 2016, pp. 44-66).

In most recent publications, Young Kim and Jung-Hoon (2019, 2022) theorized the concept of "curriculum as shadow" to convey "student learning that takes place outside schooling" (Kim & Jung-Hoon, 2019, p. 4)—that is, the unfolding that occurs beyond the formal structures of schools and classrooms. Shadow education is a by-product of the shapes and contours of this "standardized" and "measurable" social contract that students usually have to sign in to run the course of schooling—a contract that fosters competitive dispositions of survival for a hierarchical world of becoming(s). Attending to personal aspirations and fears, parents in Asia (and across the world) demand that their children take part in private tutoring services in order to improve "performance" in examinations.

Like many other practices and theories of education and schooling, "shadow education" puts our thinking, actions, and care "to test." This is, in fact, another example where the meaning(s) of love can become contradicted, contested by those who are perceived as "givers" and "receivers" of care. Thinking about the long-term wellbeing of their offspring, parents may end up (un)consciously exerting pressures on their sons and daughters to study voraciously for life-changing examinations. While parents may share hopes that this approach to parenting may support the 'intellectual development' of their offspring so they can enjoy greater levels of financial compensation, prestige, and wellbeing in the long term versus the short term, some children/youth may feel that they are unable to cope with external demands, such as the catalytic pressures of capitalism, including efficiency and accountability, to run the course of schooling. Indeed, a group of students (and researchers who examine the relationship between schooling variables and constructs such as 'test stress' and 'anxiety') may ultimately conclude that this type of parental/societal "care" may promote more (psychological) harm than good (see, for example, Putwain, 2009; Roome & Soan, 2019; Xiang et al., 2017).

Perhaps due to their social position and status, the "pushed-out" voices—the autobiographical lexis that underscore discourses of survival within the hierarchies—may not be thoroughly channeled in spaces designed for decision-making. For example, *how many illiterate individuals are able to join and effectively sustain participation in public forums?* Indeed, critical scholars commonly accept the discourse that those who navigate and shape networks of power are the individuals capable of garnering and employing "human" and "cultural capital" (see, for example, Bourdieu et al., 2021), that is, the privileged few who do not need to break intergenerational cycles of poverty to integrate "the polity." We must therefore be cautious about the types of "single thoughts" that we value, promote, and circulate within structures, in education (and beyond)—including the primacy enjoyed by evaluative systems in schools and societies.

Although the privileged few who end up benefiting from this approach of "care" may become determined to support the structures in place later in life, including the grading systems that legitimize achievement, others who struggle may or may not do so. Divergent experiences help forge public exhibitions of divergence in public debate and policy. In Post-Reconceptualization, however, I argue that curricularists should attempt to forge a nexus by "seeking unity amongst divisions" (Rocha, 2021, p. 19) while honouring the content, desires, fears, hopes, and struggles nestled and channeled through the bodies and voices that have to habituate these structures. Indeed, in my view, bringing an agglomeration of voices into a "coherent whole" where students from all walks of life may be able to unfold their subjectivities *and* flourish as citizens of a larger non-anthropocentric polity—from a fortified nexus of love towards love and justice—constitutes this Post-Reconceptualist project.

Taking part in a one-year exchange program in Japan, I participated in cross-cultural activities with Japanese students where they were asked to draw a graph depicting the ups and downs of their life trajectories, a kind of autobiographical lexis which highlighted individual and collective moments of care. Across the board, the image of graphs pointing upward and downward underscored how they individually and collectively approached their education as well as their relationship with schooling and evaluations. The meanings that I could recognize and hear from personal testimonies and the graphs were that of apprehension and anxiety—feelings conspicuously evident in the preparation for examinations and in the learning of the English language, which constitute a major policy debate in Japan, both within and outside higher educational systems (see, for example, Yonezawa et al., 2016). Of course, one can continuously deliberate about "shadow" as a public approach to education. Indeed, depending on how people position education, they can depict "shadow" as both a strength and/ or weakness. To Jung (2016), "shadow education" undermines subjectivities and, therefore, the true purpose of education. Again, the question lingers: *Can we forge convergence—a collective vision for education across con(texts)—where love is fortified, where symbiotic, relational and contextual caregiving eradicates vulnerabilities and suffering in the world?*

As I think about the concept of "shadow" in curriculum studies and about my own discussions about the "nexus of love," I am drawn to conversations with friends and loved ones, to autobiographical *moments* that make me think regressively, progressively, analytically, and synthetically about care, too. As suggested elsewhere, the world is complicated, hierarchical, and competitive—an amalgam of intertwined webs of privileged and oppressive realities. Therefore, I use the word *moments* deliberatively to highlight the fact that not all relational encounters are loving; we may not feel cared for—or willing to care for—in all moments of our lives. In *The Character of Curriculum Studies: Bildung, Currere, and the Recurring Question of the Subject*, Pinar (2011) writes: "the running of the course implies a conversation complicated with multiple interlocutors, multiple references, and temporal *moments*, as well as almost infinite possibilities, not a few of them awful" (p. xiii; emphasis added). To fortify nexus, I seek regressive and progressive moments while employing a bifocal lens to see how love circulated social structures within and across webs of privilege and oppression, webs which simultaneously altered the subject and its relationality with alterity as well as its own becoming in the world. I seek such *moments* to reverberate a more loving progression in the course—the personal and collective possibilities mentioned by Pinar which are not awful.

Studying regressively, I can focus on moments where the meanings of love were not so evident and hence question the presence of love in my life in the very course of running. This approach would certainly lead me to experience sentiments that diverge from that of love, such as that of bitterness—sentiments which we are allowed to feel sporadically, but which I argue should not constitute our situatedness of becoming in the course of development. Yet, I labor in a world of paradoxes, for I have to "work from within" (Pinar, 1972) and *still* "look outwards" to bifocalize the "self" (see CWSJL). That is, I still have to look outwards to study webs of privilege and power. *But can there be love in the webs of privilege and oppression in the world?* I believe there can be, for webs leave space for voids, and these voids can be filled by our love—or by other unloving sentiments and ways of becoming(s). When I envision love, I think, for example, of *moments* when individuals such as the Swedish Diplomat Raoul Gustaf Wallenberg issued passports to save Jews from Nazi ideological persecution; the Senegalese Captain Mbaye Diagne, who saved hundreds of lives during the genocide in Rwanda; and the people of the Chambon (see Jales Coutinho, 2022, "Forging nexus"). The tenacious work of the curricularist should be focused on these paradoxical structures, a commitment to erase webs of privilege and oppression while turning vulnerability and suffering a myth, helping our constellations of care fulfill, overflow, and ultimately replace these spaces and structures with love, the ethics of care, and its symbiotic and relational powers.

Again, this is not simple work. Most recently, as I communicated with a close friend over the phone about some of the difficulties that my "self" confronted in the course of running, she raised the distinction between love, hate, and indifference. As we exchanged words, she raised the hypothesis that the opposite of love was not hate, but indifference (probably quoting Elie Wiesel) because, when one hates, one gives attention to the subject, a trait which perhaps can be assimilated with care/giving. However, when we are indifferent to the subject, nothing that happens to it truly matters. As I dwelled on those thoughts, I realized that indifference falls outside of the nexus of love—no care, just judgementality (the tendency to judge people, cases, institutions through hard, objective criteria, usually employing the method of comparison) or glimpses of unsentimental hospitality at best. *Should we then be indifferent if we have a choice to care? Is it possible to care for and about someone by being indifferent? That is, is it possible that someone may be better cared for when s/he does not experience the effects of one's caring attention?*

I can think of many hypothetical scenarios where one may find that this is true. Think, for example, of a child who may be neglected by her mother at home. A teacher may decide that the child would be better assisted if cared for by someone else within and/or outside of the family circle. One could conclude that the mother's indifference, after having neglected the child, could make the child better off. Someone else could determine that the mother needed to be cared for, too, so that she could also care for appropriately for her child, forging and fortifying the constellations of care that we all need in the course of running—to thrive and become (loving) in the world. The mother, on the other hand, could judge that her approach to care was righteous, bringing to light information and insights that might have not been initially considered, and so on. Caring for and about "self," alterity, nature, and the cosmos is a complicated conversation and a key facet of curriculum work in a Post-Reconceptualist era.

As we labor to contribute to this "complicated conversation," I argue that we have to attempt to depart from a nexus of love, and to care for work that is "ongoing, deliberative, and autobiographical" (Jales Coutinho, 2022, p. 127). In other words, we have to remind ourselves that the voices and experiences of those who are cared for/about matter. The child feels, knows, understands... Her voice should be included as a part of her own constellation of care, as she runs the course *of* development, to collectively determine when to move the constellation to new "in-betweenness," to a new progression, analysis, and synthesis. Her voice may support theories and discourses, as well as bridge convergencies in divergencies, as people attempt to eradicate suffering and vulnerability and foster relational restorations in a collapsing world, which I posit is the true "purpose" of love. I contend that curricularists have to create ongoing momentum for democratic upbringing in our current course *of* development, listening and crediting lived experiences of becoming whilst *autobiographying* discourses and practices in/for institutional decision-making, at the personal and aggregate levels. This approach requires a new vision where decision makers no longer play with constellations of power to influence decision-making, but rather forge, strengthen, and fulfill spaces with relational, contextual care/giving through an ongoing, bifocalized study of lives within and across structures, from a fortified nexus of love.

As curricularists, we may speak of a queer ethics of care, of a BIPOC ethics of care, etc. As I espoused in CWSJL, the intersectionalities of our subjectivities are key to understanding privilege and oppression in the world. The care that a teacher may give to a BIPOC student may be greater (and different) because of intersectionalities and because of divergent lived experiences in a racist con(text). After all, a BIPOC student may be/feel more vulnerable than another child due to her lived experiences with the racist vernacular. But yet, *care must be given* (not provided, not afforded) *to all*—care which is "new, different, and yet common" (Jales Coutinho, 2022, p. 51) to those who share the classroom as they unfold to become *consciente* and loving in the world. At the end of the day, despite differences in approaches, the convergence for care is love itself... Care to learn about alterity, care to understand one's privileges, care to build a more relational world of becoming(s), a world where vulnerability and suffering constitute a myth, a place where great levels of wellbeing are shared across spectrums of diversity, where love is reverberated. We may diverge by

50 Positioning love as an ethics of care/giving in curriculum

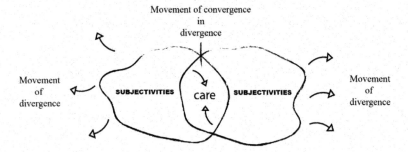

Image 3.2 Finding convergence in divergence through and with care. Created by the author.

providing greater and differentiated care to the most vulnerable, but we still converge by caring relationally and contextually *for all*. In Image 3.2, I illustrate this movement of convergence in divergence through *and* with care, as we engage in ongoing study and bifocalization to become and (re)construct the subjective "self."

We should also acknowledge that we are all prone to experiencing vulnerabilities as we position ourselves in the hierarchies of the world and experience different kinds of survivals. While some people in the bottom of the hierarchies may struggle to meet basic needs and safeguard their human dignity, others 'survive' the top of the hierarchies to maintain integrity, prestige, and recognition. The truth is, we are all surviving, in one way or another, this world of antagonistic, agonistic, and competitive becoming(s). We are all in need of care, albeit in different levels, at different capacities, as we move toward symbiosis. Undoubtedly, the world needs caregivers to make love less probabilistic and to turn it a fate for all of our humanity in this course of development.

It should be clear now that finding convergences in divergence is a paradoxical endeavour, a labor of becoming *consciente* in the world, and, most importantly, a labor of new becoming(s). Divergences exist so that we can keep pushing the boundaries of our lives and of our labor together, forging and fortifying nexus and proximity—through *and* with love—as we face paradoxes as well as hard trails in the course *of* development. For example, as we attempt to eradicate suffering and vulnerabilities in the world, we should also be willing to *become vulnerable* as we unfold our autobiographical lexis—which is perhaps one of the hardest "tasks" in returning to love in a world comprised of prisoner's dilemmas. We work in this kind of "in-betweenness" to make our work more relational and less hierarchical, especially with those individuals who do not stand in the same bases of power and privilege.

As I employ the autobiographical con(text) in the next chapter, I study love while attempting to forge and fortify nexus and proximity. I bifocalize the "self" in my study and dwell in "in-betweenness," relationally and contextually, toward a new progression and synthesis where I start to become less judgemental and more studious of relationships which are enacted through power in hierarchies, seeking to visualize, experience, and (re)position love as care/giving. At this juncture, I mobilize academic knowledge in my study primarily from the fields of psychoanalysis, psychology, and religion to understand and share my lived experiences of/with love within and across con(texts), and to advance curriculum as a "collective public moral enterprise."

I first write about my evolving relationship with my parents. I then intersect parental meanings with religious love and brotherhood love, each having a subsection in the forthcoming chapter. Finally, I deliberate on the meanings of romantic love, followed by labor love. Across all subsections, I expound how care/giving has shaped my course of running within and across con(texts) and synthesize this course of a complicated conversation from a standpoint of love, even when my own "self" and the world expect and/or demand a different kind of disposition, a different kind of becoming. Some readers may argue that these autobiographical narratives do not fully take place in formal "educational settings." Hence, they may not necessarily portray such moments as "educational experience as lived." Yet, I invite these readers to view curriculum as phenomena (re)produced by the iteration of material and discursive con(texts) which permeates not only the walls of formal educational institutions such as schools and universities, but the whole of society, "the whole of nature and the cosmos" (Jales Coutinho, 2022, p. 51). After all, the educational significance that we nurture with love, the ethics of care/giving, is intrinsically educational: it is purely an educational experience *as lived*.

References

Andrews, M. (2014). *The limits of institutional reform in development: Changing rules for realistic solutions*. Cambridge University Press.

Aoki, T. T., Pinar, W. F., & Irwin, R. L. (2012). *Curriculum in a new key: The collected works of Ted T. Aoki*. Routledge, Taylor & Francis Group.

Bourdieu, P., Champagne, P., Collier, P., Duval, J., Poupeau, F., & Rivière, M.-C. (2021). *Forms of capital*. Polity.

Bruhn, S., & Oliveira, G. (2021). Multidirectional carework across borders: Latina Immigrant Women Negotiating Motherhood and daughterhood. *Journal of Marriage and Family*, 1–22. https://doi.org/10.1111/jomf.12814

Chatzidakis, A., Hakim, J., Littler, J., Rottenberg, C., & Segal, L. (2020). *The care manifesto: The politics of interdependence*. Verso Books.

Eppert, C. (2021). Contemplating educations of ecological well-becoming, with gratitude to (mother) Earth, wildlife, and women. *Curriculum Inquiry*, *51*(3), 307–331. https://doi.org/10.1080/03626784.2021.1941797

Hall, K. F. (1996). Beauty and the beast of whiteness: Teaching race and gender. *Shakespeare Quarterly*, *47*(4), 461. https://doi.org/10.2307/2870958

Hartigan, J. (1997). Establishing the fact of Whiteness. *American Anthropologist*, *99*(3), 495–505. https://doi.org/10.1525/aa.1997.99.3.495

Haughton, N. (2004). Perceptions of beauty in Renaissance art. *Journal of Cosmetic Dermatology*, *3*(4), 229–233. https://doi.org/10.1111/j.1473-2130.2004.00142.x

Irwin, R. (2022). The 9th Education Graduate Students (EGS) Conference – Inhabiting In-betweeness. Faculty of Education – Department of Curriculum and Pedagogy. Retrieved from https://edcp.educ.ubc.ca/the-9th-education-graduate-students-egs-conference/

Jales Coutinho, A. M. (2022). *Curriculum work and social justice leadership in a post-reconceptualist era: Attaining critical consciousness and learning to become* (1st ed.). Routledge. https://doi.org/10.4324/9781003188629

Jung, J.-H. (2016). *The concept of care in curriculum studies: Juxtaposing Currere and Hakbeolism*. Routledge.

Kang, J. M. (1996). Deconstructing the ideology of white aesthetics. *Michigan Journal of Race & Law*, *2*, 283. https://repository.law.umich.edu/mjrl/vol2/iss2/3

Kim, Y. C., & Jung, J.-H. (2019). *Shadow education as worldwide curriculum studies*. Springer International Publishing.

Kim, Y. C., & Jung, J.-Hoon. (2022). *Theorizing shadow education and academic success in East Asia: Understanding the meaning, value, and use of shadow education by East Asian students*. Routledge.

Lee, N. Y. S., Wong, L. E., & Ursino, J. M. (Eds.). (2022). *Lingering with the works of Ted T. Aoki: Historical and contemporary significance for curriculum research and practice*. Routledge.

Loutzenheiser, L. W. (2014). 'who are you calling a problem?': Addressing transphobia and homophobia through school policy. *Critical Studies in Education*, *56*(1), 99–115. https://doi.org/10.1080/17508487.2015.990473

Malewski, E. (2010). Preface. In *Curriculum studies handbook – The next moment* (pp. xi–xv). Routledge.

Monk, E. P., Esposito, M. H., & Lee, H. (2021). Beholding inequality: Race, gender, and returns to physical attractiveness in the United States. *American Journal of Sociology*, *127*(1), 194–241. https://doi.org/10.1086/715141

Noddings, N. (1988). Caring. In W. F. Pinar (Ed.), *Contemporary curriculum discourses* (pp. 42–55). Peter Lang.

Oliveira, G. (2015). *Transnational care constellation: Mexican immigrant mothers and their children in Mexico and in New York City (dissertation)*. Retrieved from https://academiccommons.columbia.edu/doi/10.7916/D8RR1XBG

Oliveira, G. (2018). *Matherhood across borders: Immigrants and their children in Mexico and New York*. New York University Press.

Oliveira, G. (2020). Transnational care constellations: IM/migrant families, children and Education. *Crossings: Journal of Migration & Culture, 11*(2), 187–199. https://doi.org/10.1386/cjmc_00024_1

Oscarson, C. (2019). Dominion in the anthropocene. *Dialogue: A Journal of Mormon Thought, 52*(4), 1–16. https://doi.org/10.5406/dialjmormthou.52.4.0001

Osmond-Johnson, P., & Turner, P. (2020). Navigating the "ethical space" of truth and reconciliation: Non-indigenous school principals in Saskatchewan. *Curriculum Inquiry, 50*(1), 54–77. https://doi.org/10.1080/03626784.2020.1715205

Owis, B. (2022). Queering and trans-gressing care: towards a queer ethics of care in QTBIPOC Education. Unpublished Dissertation. https://bishopowis.com

Painter, N. I. (2011). *The history of white people*. W. W. Norton & Company.

Peters, M. A. (2015). Why is my curriculum white? *Educational Philosophy and Theory, 47*(7), 641–646. https://doi.org/10.1080/00131857.2015.1037227

Piepzna-Samarasinha, L. L. (2018). *Care work: Dreaming disability justice*. Arsenal Pulp Press.

Pinar, W. F. (1972, January). Working from within. *Educational Leadership*, 29(4), 329–331.

Pinar, W. F. (2011). *Character of curriculum studies: Bildung, currere, and the recurring question of the subject*. Palgrave Macmillan.

Pinar, W. F. (2015). *Educational experience as lived: Knowledge, history, alterity: The selected works of William F. Pinar* (1st ed.). Routledge. https://doi.org/10.4324/9781315752594

Pinar, W. F., & Grumet, M. R. (1976). *Toward a poor curriculum*. Kendall & Hunt.

Pinar, W. F., Reynolds, W. M., Slattery, P., & Taubman, P. M. (1995). *Understanding curriculum: An introduction to the study of historical and contemporary curriculum discourses*. Peter Lang.

Popkewitz, T. S. (2009). Curriculum study, curriculum history, and curriculum theory: The reason of Reason. *Journal of Curriculum Studies, 41*(3), 301–319. https://doi.org/10.1080/00220270902777021

Putwain, D. W. (2009). Assessment and examination stress in key stage 4. *British Educational Research Journal, 35*(3), 391–411. https://doi.org/10.1080/01411920802044404

Rocha, S. (2021). *Syllabus as curriculum: A reconceptualist approach*. Routledge.

Roome, T., & Soan, C. A. (2019). GCSE exam stress: Student perceptions of the effects on wellbeing and performance. *Pastoral Care in Education, 37*(4), 297–315. https://doi.org/10.1080/02643944.2019.1665091

Salmón, E. (2000). Kincentric ecology: Indigenous perceptions of the human-nature relationship. *Ecological Applications, 10*(5), 1327–1332. https://doi.org/10.2307/2641288

Styres, S. D. (2017). *Pathways for remembering and recognizing indigenous thought in education: Philosophies of iethinihsténha ohwentsiakékha (land)*. University of Toronto Press.

Tuck, E. (2009). Suspending damage: A letter to communities. *Harvard Educational Review, 79*(3), 409–428. https://doi.org/10.17763/haer.79.3.n0016675661t3n15

UBC Botanical Garden. (2021, August 25). *Nitobe memorial garden*. UBC Botanical Garden. Retrieved March 27, 2022, from https://botanicalgarden.ubc.ca/visit/nitobe-memorial-garden/

Varga, B. A., & Shear, S. (2022). Flows of anti-colonialism: (re)configurations and emplotments of more-than-witness(es/ing) in the an(thropo/glo)cene. *Journal of Curriculum and Pedagogy*, 1–22. https://doi.org/10.1080/15505170.2022.2107585

Wang, H. (2013). A nonviolent perspective on internationalizing curriculum studies. In W. Pinar (Ed.), *International handbook of curriculum research* (2nd ed., pp. 67–76). Routledge.

Weis, L., & Fine, M. (2012). Critical bifocality and circuits of privilege: Expanding critical ethnographic theory and design. *Harvard Educational Review,82*(2),173–201.https://doi.org/10.17763/haer.82.2.v1jx34n441532242

Xiang, Z., Tan, S., Kang, Q., Zhang, B., & Zhu, L. (2017). Longitudinal effects of examination stress on psychological well-being and a possible mediating role of self-esteem in Chinese high school students. *Journal of Happiness Studies, 20*(1), 283–305. https://doi.org/10.1007/s10902-017-9948-9

Yonezawa, A., Kitamura, Y., Meerman, A., & Kuroda, K. (Eds.). (2016). *Emerging international dimensions in East Asian higher education*. Springer.

4 Unfolding autobiographies, fortifying love in curriculum

Running the course and seeking con(texts) to bifocalize the 'self' regressively, progressively, analytically, and synthetically, curricularists are invited to unfold greater levels of *conscientização* and exert their critical agencies to change the course of development itself. So, instead of holding hegemonic understandings of 'self'—a single thought which may halt a critical understanding of how such con(texts) (re)produce and enable different levels of agency and freedoms in the course of one's development, relationally and contextually, one bifocalizes the self within and across con(texts) to understand the complex relationships that one's "self" has inherited from historical constructions of the 'other'—"relations of the past that are yet present, internal and external to one another, paradoxically within and beyond sight" (Jales Coutinho, 2022, p. 34).

For example, when one seeks within a con(text) in a regressive moment (e.g., racial), one attempts to understand how Whiteness as a racial con(text) evolved throughout the course of development to constitute a facet of one's becoming *in relation to* Blackness. One can also seek across contexts (e.g., geographical and technological) to deepen such qualitative understanding. For example, *what has been the construction and experiences of Whiteness as racial con(text) in relation to my experiences of becoming within and across the geographical con(texts) of Brazil, the United States, Japan, and Canada? How could it be related to other aesthetic con(texts) which I have not yet experienced?*

For those who are acquainted with the fictional series of *Harry Potter*, the act of "seeking contexts" regressively would be tantamount to one's use of the *pensieve*, a magical device where characters would place and revisit memories and histories from the past—histories that would still be present in one's lived circumstances of becoming. In the *pensieve*, subjects would contemplate the past in order to study these events in an "analytical moment." Likewise, the progression could be

DOI: 10.4324/9781003359968-4

tantamount to the *time turner*, a device where individuals would be able to see and contemplate the (un)foreseeable future. Regressively and progressively, individuals are brought to the analytical moment where they can mobilize academic knowledge to study these experiences and the circuits of privilege and power that constitute them before synthesizing these in their lexis of becoming. This is the moment, the place from where the subject can attempt to critically change, in solitude and with others, the course of events which may lead him/her to a certain progression in the course *of* development—a moment where love *can* be genesis, and where relationality overthrows power and, consequently, privilege and oppression—forging novel histories, memories, and autobiographical understandings for becoming.

Of course, "returning to love" while running the very course of development is *no* simple undertaking. I humbly attempt to take some steps in that direction in my own unfolding, but I admit that this is *ongoing labor*, for we can be perfect but yet so ever *in*complete, the very synthesis of a complicated conversation. In other words, "returning to love" is not necessarily a linear process; it could be interpreted as a cyclical commitment to study and to approach love and justice. After all, the very act of "seeking contexts" implicates the study of novel "data" from self and world which may lead people to engage in ongoing study, which in turn may culminate in forms of solidarity and negotiation and/or love and proliferation… In sum, the ethical commitment involved in autobiographical inquiry toward love as genesis (and reconciliation) is a course, and yet a complicated one. Although such complicatedness (e.g. matters pertaining to truth, memory, forgiveness, anger, etc.) might be/come the focus of other projects, I purposefully decided to focus this book on the study and fortification of love as an ethics of care/giving because of its primacy in curriculum work as a collective public moral enterprise.

Seeking con(texts) while bifocalizing the "self" in my *currere*, the love(s) and meanings that I ascribe to the following autobiographical excerpts are interconnected, unfolding continuously in divergent and converging moments, in "in-betweenness," as I face the shapeless, ever-changing contours of these complicated conversations—conversations that evolve(d) both concomitantly and chronologically throughout the course of time, throughout the contours of space in regressive, progressive, analytical, and synthetical moments. Altogether, they forge a short autobiographical lexis of/for/about love as an ethics of care/giving. I bifocalize the "self" within and across con(texts), in relation to subjects (e.g., parents, God, brother, dating individuals, and colleagues) and subjectified objects (e.g., cards, the Bible, rocking chair, umbrella, and pencils), and uncover hidden meanings that might have not been so apparent at first glance. Finally, I conclude this chapter by sharing some thoughts about convergences in and through care in curriculum as a "collective public moral enterprise."

4.1 Parental love

Embraced by love, I was conceived and started to walk, and then to run, unaware that one day I would rise to see the world from the top of mountains. While I was still exchanging direct fluids inside my mother's womb, she labored to craft ornaments for children's parties. She was gifted with manual, crafting work, demonstrating her inner ability to forge delicacy, create gossamer, and give care. Throughout breastfeeding, my mother nourished me, exchanging fluids whilst gifting me biological means for protection and survival so that I could thrive in a viral world. My father carried me in his arms, too. Learning continuously about their stories of survival, I realize that this has been a long journey, longer than my own memory can recall.

Having departed her homeland and having already experienced the many facets of motherhood in her teenage years, my mother now cared for two young boys in the *favelas* of Rio de Janeiro. With my father, we lived in a small dwelling made of wood and cardboard. During the harsh days of summer, she continuously brought the two newborns, which had been conceived within a year of one another, to experience the cooling waters of an old bucket—I am not aware of our sanitary conditions back then, or whether or not we even had running water. I learned that work was scarce, but they had a great drive to live, a trait which I believe they shared with their own parents.

Despite the difficulties of living in a chaotic and unequal world, care constituted my situatedness of becoming. Growing up, I joined the world of schooling whilst travelling between cities as my father labored in his new, formal managerial work, which demanded constant moves. Initially, I was scared of schools, of being left in the hand of strangers by my mother. I cried often. Despite overall challenges with transitions, somehow my parents, together with my brother and I, were able to survive the daily grind, making their way back to our homeland, in the Northeast region, where our story continued to unfold at school and amongst the larger units of our Brazilian family.

Starting in primary school, I began to cherish the caregiving that I witnessed and experienced when female teachers looked after my well-being, and vice versa. I believe that, at that point, I began to associate the role of teaching with the caring sentiments I had already forged and nurtured with motherhood. I started to become accustomed to new places, to learn to be cared for by teachers. That was when I was able to stop crying after being left at school: when I felt embraced by the kind of love I experienced at home. Admiring and now associating teaching with motherhood—a type of relationship that is well examined in Madeleine Grumet's *Bitter Milk: Women and Teaching*—, I became open to new becomings.

Yet, the paradoxical also confronted me because I grew to learn to be ashamed of being a "have-not." While the care I received could be perceived as a privilege in a world of vulnerabilities, I remember that I began *to compare* my life with that of my peers. As a young child, the care which I experienced did not seem to surpass the comparative meanings that constituted my situatedness of becoming at school. While I began to admire my teachers and I wanted to please them, I also started to observe what other children were offered—and what I was *not*. Care seems to be somehow dissolved in a world of comparative becomings, for I started to navigate between the relational and the comparative, in this new kind of "in-betweenness."

Meanwhile, at home, observing the daily struggle and now having to support my family in our now informal *cantina* named after *São Francisco* (English: Saint Francis)—*cantina* is a small community market where people sell fruits, vegetables, and all sorts of delicacies and products—, I started to give care by cleaning the house to help my mother, too. After noticing that my mother would arrive late after a day of work, I decided to wash the dishes; that constituted my first household chore. After arriving home, and noticing her smile when she saw the empty sink, I continued to do this and other household chores, such as sweeping the house. These activities became predominant when my brother fell sick, battling to survive appendicitis and an infection in his body. Looking after him at the hospital for weeks and months, my mother seemed more absent from my life. In a written letter I compiled with the help of a cousin, I told my mom I would want to become a physician in order to care for our family—a profession that I cannot practice, but a promise (to care) that I still hope to fulfill. My brother ended up surviving the health battle with an expansive and glowing constellation of care, and I survived some moments of loneliness. He was winning in terms of strength.

At this time, parental and family love is what kept us afloat. Religion also seemed to fortify close-to-mourning spirits. All my family was Catholic back then. Despite being a country full of *machismos*, Brazil is also known for being a matriarchal and religious society (see Kottak, 2019). Our family was therefore structured to live in webs of religion, matriarch, and *machismo*, "in-betweens" fulfilled with love—and I would say with hints of systemic oppression, too. My father and all of her sons paid so much respect to my grandmother—certainly a *nordestina* who survived many adversities—but they also enjoyed many privileges, for only the females would be responsible to care for household chores before her.

While the women would stay in the kitchen cooking and preparing delicacies, the men would usually stay outside, drinking, conversing, and playing cards, especially during festive periods. My father and other family members seemed to enjoy that care, for they received it with great delight—perhaps as a way to forget the much harsher realities lingering outside of the family bubble. Similarly, my grandmother demonstrated that she enjoyed to give that kind of care, too. Yet I am unsure how the other ladies perceived those chores, which meanings *they* attributed to the objects and subjects as they collectively forged those complex relational moments. *How did my aunts feel and what did they think in relation to their brothers, husbands, and sons?* Growing up, I began to dislike my father's card playing, especially when I longed for care, too.

At some point much later in life, he listened. But when I was young, I began *to compare* how much care one person gave to the other, especially within the household. I was attentive to my father's way of caring, and also to that of my mother. They certainly cared for our survival. That I cannot doubt. They certainly brought with them their own scars as they attempted to bridge several "in-between" feelings and memories of motherhood and fatherhood care, especially when conflict arose within the larger family. I am more studious of such relationships now as I attempt to run this course of a complicated conversation, but back then all I could do was to be judgemental. *How could people within the family diverge so much in their approaches to care?* I constantly thought, becoming disappointed and frustrated when I did not see people care for one another as much as I thought they should have. That was my perception of reality.

Years later, speaking with a Brazilian policymaker, I was told that it is within the family that we learn to live with difference and appreciate diversity. I wish I had shared that understanding as a child, for I was too focused on divergences, forgetting the forces that attempted to forge convergencies in my life at the time, the appreciation which is also responsible for holding constellations of care together. I was not fully aware of and did not thoroughly study, as an academic endeavour, all the possible external influences—circuits of privilege and oppression—that made people act as they did. That is, I did not think critically *and* relationally of people's upbringing and traumas, including my father's (I still know very little about their autobiographies. I believe they conversed and read very little with/to us as children due to responsibilities and other endeavours). As I have alluded to in CWSJL, it would be during my experience in the United States, during a course about poverty in America, and later in Japan, when I learned about the effects of toxic stress on the brain (see, for example, World Bank, 2015), that I would begin to think of these relations a little bit more relationally whilst learning about the artifacts of governmentality.

Over time, as a child and as a youth, I was drawn to the arms of motherhood because I appreciated all the care that my mother was able to give, especially when nexus and proximity no longer seemed to constitute our situatedness of becoming in the family. At some point, parental love no longer lingered in the "in-between." Relationality did not seem to permeate the unfolding because competition constituted the unfolding then. My brother and I were called upon to choose one course or the other. Living that experience, I despised the dichotomy: at this time, it would be either *this* or *that*. Now, it felt like I played cards, too. I could show either a heart or a sword, a "game" where there could be just one single "outcome," one disparate lived experience of becoming.

4.2 Religious love

Throughout my brother's illness, religion sustained the family, especially its senior members. The tenets of Catholicism regulated all of our worship. I had practiced religious rituals since infancy, and such events came to strengthen the faith of the family. My relationship with the divine was mostly connected to these rituals and to attending the Sunday religious ceremonies with my brother. Each week we had breakfast early and headed to church where we would also read the recondite liturgy to a small, quiet audience. My evolving (and limited) understanding of the divine was confined to the abstruse readings of the Bible. That huge book would provide answers to the grown-ups on how to run the course. As part of the rituals, I spoke in private with the priest to confess my sins, and in a kind response he asked me to deliver a few prayers after the ceremonies. My relationship with and my understanding of God were circumscribed by the following overarching notion: humankind is prone to committing sins, and so we should ask for forgiveness through prayers, and be vigilant to not commit them in the course of running.

Living in my own bubble and having no contact with people of other religions, I had no idea about the existence of other people and rituals, such as Muslims and Islam—until I began to be exposed to the complex discourses against terrorism in the years that followed 9/11. At that time, I also thought that the divine would only help us forge a path to heaven. But such an understanding would suddenly change, for the divine—or the persons who spoke of God—could also promote some divergencies. Having to handle and negotiate the responsibilities of work and motherhood, my mother decided to bring someone into the house to care for us while she had to deal with work responsibilities in our small *cantina*. That lady was also a Christian, but she provided another understanding of the Bible. She was a Protestant and she preached her views to us, and we listened. Over time, we began to appreciate her discourses and to attend a Protestant church where acceptance for saints was disregarded. My father, however, remained committed to Catholicism. Accordingly, our lives changed forever.

A strict kind of 'religious love,' an attachment for specific understandings mixed with what I now recognize as hints of *machismo* and *patriarch* led to the dismemberment of the family. Calls for divorce were uttered. My life began to become separated just like the church in 1517 when Martin Luther promoted the Reformation in Europe (Mullett, 2015). As life got less and less centered on 'unitary' ways of becomings, seemingly diverging without attempting to converge, I also began to learn about other religions in school. Attending the state school where my "self" and society would attribute meanings to the school uniform (see CWSJL, Chapter 3), I began to learn about diversity in religion.

I remember that my primary school teacher also shared with her students the tenets of Christianity, but she was open-minded in her approach to religious education. She brought to us texts that revealed how other peoples practiced their religions in other corners of the world. Studying the interactions regressively, I remember that she brought texts about religious practices in India, a country where various deities are worshiped, so that we could see our world in big(ger) terms. However, my own lived experience with/of religion remained constrained to the "self," for I never felt comfortable to share in the classroom what happened in my (religious) life back then. The complicated conversations that evolved were only based on those texts, never on my experiences of becoming.

Over time and after the divorce, my father attempted to bring me and my brother to religious ceremonies at the Catholic church, coming to pick us up every Sunday morning. I disliked this experience because

I no longer felt connected to the church. Whereas my mother desired that we accompanied her to evening celebrations—she would invite us to join her to the church now and then—, my father seemed to want to impose his will on us, a kind of divergence that ended up distancing my "self" from the divine, and the church altogether—be it Protestant or not. As a youth, and now no longer an attendee of religious celebrations, I would go to the church rarely, only to appreciate special ceremonies such as that of marriage. My connection with the divine had been severed, but I maintained my connection with my father, who would, a few years later, forge another constellation of care whilst attempting to connect and care more assiduously for his family.

In my later international experiences I would meet individuals that practiced either several other religions, or none. I was pleased that we would make connections in spite of differences. I learned through friendship in college and elsewhere that convergence could exist in a world of conflictuous becoming(s), that people from different context(s) could care, share a table, and be happy altogether. Of course, my knowledge of world religions is still relatively poor, but my interest in how people celebrate care in various religions is burgeoning, and so is my desire to understand how different societies intersect "care" as well as concepts such as "privilege" and "oppression" in curriculum, broadly speaking, and in its school subjects. Just like indigeneity, there is still so much to study, to learn, to unfold. There is so much nexus and proximity to forge as a part of this Post-Reconceptualist endeavour as a collective public moral enterprise.

In Canada, I ended up enrolling in a religious course at the University of Toronto where the instructor and the students grew critical of how religious education was delivered across the world. One of the most interesting questions arose when we addressed the question of secularity (see, for example, Patrick, 2015; Stafford, 2016). Speaking with his students, the instructor questioned whether the secularization of schools could not be considered "indoctrination" too. He raised the question more or less in these lines: *Do we not also attempt to 'indoctrinate' students by teaching them about market mechanisms?* I was brought regressively to a time where I learned about the microeconomic behaviour/concepts of the small firm. Indeed, we definitely teach students to perceive the world through supply and demand curves. Although my colleagues and I collectively perceived some questions through a technicist approach (see CWSJL, "Informed Dialogue: Perceiving curriculum—and everything else—as objects," Chapter 4), religious education helped me see curriculum studies as a complicated conversation, too.

I have recently begun to study in order to (re)connect my "self" with the divine—the spiritual—and to better understand how "love" and "the divine" itself are positioned in various religious texts. While in infanthood the Bible would characterize the sacred object from which grownups would retrieve lessons on how to run the course, now I see that several religions/religious texts can contribute to this enterprise. My conclusion is that we need to teach students that *divergencies* exist in the world, in terms of worship and prayer, just as an example, but that we can still *converge* in approaches to care *across religions*—that we can become spiritually and physically connected through and with care/giving, that is, that we can collectively care about/for the "self," alterity, nature, and the cosmos at all corners of the world. Dwelling in the in-between helps me to pose the following question: *Can people celebrate care and convergencies through religion studies in democratic institutions such as schools?*

I conclude that if we are going to teach students about religions, we should attempt to teach them about how religions approach and teach care, how we can become more caring toward our "selves" and our "neighbours" within and beyond our own religion, in our own spirituality, whilst minimizing divisions to promote some convergence, to reverberate love within *and* beyond schools. I therefore join other members of a scholarly community who contend that religious education may be beneficial (if not essential) to students in a polity (see, for example, Noddings, 2008). Indeed, I argue that such an education may not necessarily contradict democratic tenets, but rather forge another nexus for curriculum (and society): one wherein caregiving, knowledge, and spiritual awakening constitute curriculum-as-lived.

As I continue to seek context(s) to bifocalize the self, I am always drawn to how people demonstrate care toward one another. I know now that it is not only possible to seek such convergencies to forge nexus with friends and loved ones in the course of running, but also in texts such as the Torah, the New Testament, and the Quran, to name just a few. Of course, even within religions, divergence in meaning(s) and traditions exist. For example, in Islam, just like in Christianity, there exists a diversity between Sunni and Shia groups, each having "diverse schools of theology and law" (Esposito, 2011, p. 3). As a person who speaks about religions without enjoying the status of a "specialist" in each, I am cautious to draw many conclusions at this present moment about religious texts and practices generally. Yet, I still seek to envision —in my humble attempt to connect with the divine and in my quest to bifocalize— how I can celebrate and practice caregiving in my relational encounters *with* beloved others from across the large spectrum of world religions. This is part of the unfolding, of my self-awakening.

Attempting to understand a little bit better the *meanings of care* in the Quran and in other religious texts, I have now spent some mornings and afternoons engaging my "self" relationally and contextually in and through these sacred readings. In the Quran, some passages reverberate the 'true' meaning of the revelations (See, for example, Quran, Chapter 3, ◊7; Chapter 5, ◊12)—the words which had once been delivered by the prophet Muhammad ibn Abdullah, and which constitute the sacred book for Muslims, containing religious, political, and moral codes. Possessing 114 chapters, the Quran positions God in diverse discourses: God is loving, wise, generous, forgiving, just, protecting, observant, severe in punishment, etc. (See, for example, Quran, Chapter 2, ◊192–◊196; Chapter 8, ◊69–◊71). I reckon that religious scholars and practitioners can raise several relevant questions about how these and other positionings may or may not contradict one another, and how they can converge to forge "a whole," that is, a cohesive and (yet) evolving understanding of the religion of Islam as a loving, public, and collective enterprise.

The meanings we attribute to God may indeed be various. We may see God and her/his mighty in various objects and encounters. S/he might not have a face to some people, or his/her name might not be pronounced, but to others s/he might… As I start to pay closer attention to spirituality and study how religion can be cherished in curriculum, I am drawn to my encounters with nature and to indigenous ways of knowing, too. Once I started to recognize the love and fortify its meanings in my life, I was able to see the divine and his/her mighty and presence, for love exists even in the air we breathe. After all, the divine has gifted us this and other wonders so that our lives could thrive and unfold in this planet. Caregiving exists in nature, and we are part of this symbiotic act, even if we no longer recognize or position our complicated selves in these overflowing, relational moments of love with alterity, nature, and the cosmos. In the course of development, we might have lost some of our capacity to seek the convergence that bounds, the caregiving that heals (historical) wounds. As curricularists, we are therefore called upon to seek these relational aspects of being/becoming that we might have left behind in the course *of* development.

Further, we can study how moments, ideas, and practices of caregiving (in Islam and in other religions) intersect with one another relationally, and how these can support spiritual attunement with the divine throughout the course of running. Some critical scholars can raise the question: *Would this not be tantamount to an "euphemism of secularization"* (Barlas, 2013, p. 420) *of religions?* I would argue otherwise.

Contemplating and cherishing religions as loving, spiritual phenomena—a collective public moral enterprise that is able to lift individuals through love, especially those who, for one reason or another, are vulnerable and do not feel cared for by the course of running—may bring religions *together* to forge a nexus for curriculum, shaping its contours for personal and collective self-awakening: the meaningful bridges that we can create with "self," alterity, and the divine, as well as with nature and the larger cosmos, for new becomings.

Indeed, seeking a cohesive and (yet) evolving understanding of religion, a studious and reflexive undertaking, would be possible in any denomination, not only in Islam—*as long as people are willing to engage in complicated conversations by departing from a nexus of love, aiming to fortify it*. This work would undoubtedly require some deliberations on: (i) the hermeneutic role of interpretations—shifting from a "religious hermeneutics of violence" (Rowley & Wild-Wood, 2017) toward a "religious hermeneutics of love"—, and (ii) on the "monolithic views" attributed to faiths/religions such as Islam, and their evolving approaches to educational leadership (Brooks & Mutohar, 2018), just as an example. Indeed, although I speak from a position of a non-practitioner/non-specialist of Islam (but as a person who currently *relates with it*), I see that ramifications grounded on critical readings exist in the expansive, educational, religious, and cultural scholarship (see, for example, Duderija, 2020; Niyozov, 2010).

I argue that, in Post-Reconceptualization, such scholarship and practices need to embrace discussions and principles grounded on relational and contextual *caregiving*. Based on the work of indigenous scholars, I concluded in CWSJL (see Chapter 2) that such conversations must first take place among those who practice the religion as they *collectively* find a voice to represent themselves to alterity, that is, to the larger public (see, for example, Barlas, 2013)—thus helping shift the "talk-on-behalf-of-and-about" scheme to "talking-back" to "talking-with." As we dwell *with others* upon that bridge, as we learn to "talk with," we may be able to run the course of this complicated conversation *with* those who aspire to build a more relational and contextual world of becomings to actualize this project of curriculum as a collective public moral enterprise. In Post-Reconceptualization, deliberative and autobiographical forums must become more prevalent as curricularists come together to forge nexus and to make this complicated conversation *ours*—from and towards a fortified nexus of love.

Not surprisingly, other fields such as the fields of "comparative law" have attempted to forge nexus (see Twining, 2009) so that scholars can have a more expansive understanding of codes within and across cultures as a part of their institutional con(text). In the Post-Reconceptualization era of curriculum studies, which encompasses the mobilization of knowledge from diverse fields, including law, the actualization of a new form of "relational studies" may support this intellectual and collective labor within schools, too. Indeed, I believe this is just one of the many relational and contextual discussions we have to undertake as curricularists if we aspire to share and celebrate a caregiving future across differences—that is, if curriculum is to support the unfolding akin to "learn to become."

4.3 Brotherhood love

My relationship with my brother was characterized by conflicts. After falling sick and recovering, attention was primarily given to him. While I attempted to support my mother by doing household chores, my brother was protected from taking part in such 'responsibilities'– he was just given 'light' work, I thought. Back then, I did not believe I disputed attention from my mother and father. I rather nurtured a strong sentiment of injustice and dislike, for he did not seem to appreciate taking those 'responsibilities' for himself. I believed that my parents over-protected him. More often than not, "judgementality" dominated my ways of thinking when I thought of brotherhood *and* alterity. The 'judgementality' severed relationships.

Over time, my brother and I grew up to share the same house, but we ended up conversing very little with one another, especially as we entered our teenage years. Accepted to study at a prestigious technical school, we ended up spending one year in different educational environments, until I was accepted in that same school one year later. Afraid of failure (I had heard from him how challenging his freshman year in high school had been), I studied voraciously and spent basically the entire day at school seeking help to overcome what we usually call "educational gaps" or "historical debts" (see Ladson-Billings, 2006).

As we laboured to overcome such "gaps," my brother and I spent very little time together. We basically arrived home in the end of the afternoon or in the evening. We struggled to learn curriculum subjects such as English and Chemistry. My mother, now "the head" of the house, attempted to care for us by expanding her services in her small salon. We began to struggle financially. In that freshman year, as I headed back from a lake near the beach to meet my father for a family reunion, I heard my brother whisper something to himself for the first time. "How strange," I thought. Time passed. A few months later, and now at home with my mother, I saw my brother sitting and rocking in the chair in the kitchen. He had a blue pencil and a notebook on his hand where he would write voraciously, speak to himself, and scribble his own writing uninterruptedly. I got afraid.

My mother surely did not know what was happening then. She sought help and found support with a psychologist from her church. Although I am not able to speak for my brother about his experiences of becoming, I felt greater responsibilities being placed on my shoulder as a seemingly new illness began to delineate the dynamics within the household. Stress and apprehension took over our days and nights. Our understanding of his illness was wanting. It took time for us to comprehend the complexity of the situation—and how we could best care for him, something that we continuously have to do as we learn with *and* from him about his experiences of becoming, while centering and bridging this knowledge with his community of caregivers, and with those who are considered 'specialists,' who named his condition a "psychotic disorder." After all, caring for and about can be a complicated conversation, but in this complicatedness, some convergence is forged through *and* with love as a form of genesis. As I have alluded to in CWSJL, genesis is important in/for complicated conversations, for those people who labor and for whose lives are shaped by complexity, the multiple and intertwined context(s) that constitute the facets of becoming(s) in the world.

During those trying times, I began to seek help at school to support our household financially, too. I ended up joining an apprenticeship program for low-income students. The experiences I lived at home helped me fortify the love that I had nurtured for my mother, and to see that, despite earlier divergencies, the constellation which had stood for my brother once was still there caring for his wellbeing. That was a relief. We moved on, somehow, as new episodes such as that of the rocking chair happened over the years. The fight was ongoing, sometimes tiresome. I realized that, despite constellations of care, my brother's strength was bound to break, that we are bound to break now and then; that care is paramount to new becoming(s) in a world that craves (or have to crave) for *collective* healing—human and ecological.

As a youth, I tried to push myself harder to care for and about my brother's situatedness of becoming. Surprisingly, however, I was still judgemental, but now for other reasons: my brother started to take stands against his medication, especially in college when he was able to mobilize more kinds of academic knowledge to understand his situatedness of becoming. I certainly did not have a well-developed 'bifocal' vision then, for I usually perceived my own location of 'normalcy' as a parameter to judge his decision-making. How hard for me was *to relate* with his suffering over the years, perhaps to my own fault. My love seemed to wane, my privilege barely allowing me to look at *and* study *his* reality of the lived experience of his condition. He would later tell me some of the terrifying visions he had when his mind tricked him, lived experiences that are hard to study, let alone *to live*. He began to share things with our family, including the film *A Beautiful Mind* directed by Ron Howard—a movie which lingers in my mind till this present day—, perhaps as a way to ask for help, to achieve a better collective understanding.

My brother grew more interested in the fields of social work and psychology, but in doing so he grew critical of the industries and of the persons who relied heavily on pharmaceuticals to give care. While I acknowledge and agree that industries are not always focused on *collective* care, usually interested in maximizing profits by creating, for example, monopolies, I still attempt to bridge this more holistic view of caring with one where people can benefit from the ethical contributions of pharmaceutical industry—this, of course, constitutes another quest for individuals who labor in the intersections of health care, wellbeing, and policymaking (see, for example, Independent, 2019). There is still so much to study and to unfold in this complicated and often unjust world of hierarchical, competitive, and antagonistic becoming(s)—a world that increasingly defies our collective mental health.

My brother's own craving for independence allowed him to complete his undergraduate program and to seek a more holistic understanding of his evolving condition—to understand his "condition" in relation to his unfolding and situatedness of becoming. I believe 'independence' and 'self-determination' have constituted some of the critical words which he employs in his unfolding autobiographical vernacular—unwilling to be told what to do, but to have a say on how he can also care for himself, as an individual in his own right, as a part of a collective who gives care. It becomes clearer to me that receiving is also, in fact, a part of giving. When someone accepts caregiving with *and* from love, that person is giving care, too—a symbiotic event. I thank my brother for giving care, and for allowing my "self" to see my unfolding in relation to his. I thank my brother for allowing me to give, too, even when the world, my rocking-chair apprehension, and my own "self" expect and/or demand a different kind of disposition, a different kind of feeling, a different kind of becoming.

4.4 Romantic love

I was born to have some platonic loves. Attracted to a few individuals who demonstrated care, I began to understand that I would live in the world of queer later in my teenage years. One of these individuals was able to steal my heart in ways that I could not foresee, however. We agreed to go to the beach once, as friends. Looking at the blue sky and having not yet fully understood what would soon unfold, we held hands, we kissed, and we departed... At the bus stop, he hugged me, and over the course of the months, our proximity grew. Our close friends noticed it first, and sometime later people out of our inner circle.

Excited to be able to fulfill a dream and head to the United States to earn my Bachelor's degree, I did not image what romantic love would do to me. Some months prior to my departure, I looked at raindrops leave their marks on the glassed windows of the bus, as I headed home, contemplative, holding in my hands an umbrella. In a sudden snap, I remembered that he was feeling quite unwell earlier in the day, so I got off the bus and headed towards his direction; he had no umbrella with him. Meeting him sometime later at his work station at twilight, I accompanied him to the bus stop. The rain fell softly on us. At this time, overcoming the apprehension of public love display, I held my umbrella gently over him as he embraced me. My willingness *to return* and to give him my care was greater than my own "self." I loved him *profoundly*. I believed he did, too.

My capacity to return, our willingness to hold each other, that kept us together. 'Heading back' became our ritual as we attempted to see each other at school, until I would be able to do it for "the last time." A few hours before taking my flight to the United States, I told my mother I would head back to school to say my farewells. She did not understand my urgent call, but she realized that that would be important to me. And, so, I went. He and I met and we sat under a huge cashew tree in front of the soccer court, looking at the same sky which had once greeted our love some months earlier in the beach. Laying his head on my shoulder, he told me that it was almost time for me to leave, and so I went, broken-hearted. I know he felt the same way too.

In the United States, struggling to adapt to college life, we chatted sporadically, for I was unable to give him the attention I think I should have had. Toward the summer, I attempted a re-approximation, but he no longer seemed that attached. Yet, I loved him. Feeling distressed due to more than one event, I started to do cross-country running and change my ways of becoming. The mountains, the glories of nature, and later some great friendship helped me see the course, its vivid colours and shapes, a little bit more differently. I felt cared for by nature when I could not fully care for my "self." Meanwhile, I looked at the sky to search for stars, to feel love's light. Darkness could not take over me. I still cared for and about loved ones, and about *him*.

Collecting funds to return home after a year and a half, I attempted a re-approximation in Brazil, again. At this time, we made plans to meet in the *same* beach; we ended up looking at the *same* blue sky some days after. We held hands once again, we kissed, and we departed... surprisingly, a few days later, in what I perceived as a cold gesture, he uttered his farewells to me. At this time, under a bright moon light, at the *same* bus stop I had once accompanied him with my umbrella, I was left truly empty-handed. The moon said his good-byes to me, and so, in a way, I was told to carry on, to survive my own "self." Back then, I did not tell him about the deep sadness that I carried within me because I did not think it was fair to him; I feared that he would blame himself had he come to know. Enjoying another opportunity to return home before heading to Japan, we no longer met, but I still felt deeply for him. I felt deeply for my "self."

In Japan, feeling a little bit better about the course, I enjoyed greater moments of solitude. On my lonely walks and runs, I observed couples, and I attempted to date again. I gave my "self" the opportunity to be with a lovely half-Japanese guy I had met, but I gave up dating because we—perhaps my judgementality more than him—were not able to sustain convergence. I also crossed streets observing the overall trust that people shared with one another. At a glance, I saw a particular Japanese gentleman standing, waiting for a lady who crossed a street. As I observed, he raised his hand, reaching hers and holding it tightly. They walked together as if only death could set them apart. I looked at my own hand and I found it empty as if love had never touched it. My eyes inevitably stared at the floor as my thoughts immersed me in confusing idle memories. I looked at the couple again as they walked away. Everything I could do—besides taking this picture (Image 4.1)—was to experience a glimpse of happiness for them, for love had clearly touched their hands, hearts, and souls. They turned the corner and I opened a broad smile. I stared at my empty hands and I turned back with nothing to hold, but my own memories.

My Japanese, scholarly experience in Nagoya Shi assured me that my quest for knowledge would need to overturn my desire to embrace "romantic love" if I aimed to continue fulfilling my dreams. I started to long for "the what" more than for "the heart," or at least I thought I did. At that point, I reckoned that there would be no longer

Image 4.1 Japanese couple holding hands, walking in one of the streets of Nagoya-shi.

Photographed by the author.

"in-betweenness." However, completing my undergraduate program and returning home, I ended up meeting him again. This time he looked deep into my eyes and vowed his long-term, non-negotiable romantic love to me, but his promises would soon be broken—love would not (be) fulfill(ed).

Unfortunately, over time, I ended up hurting him too, in ways that he might not even expected—actions that ultimately served to hurt my own "self"—and, for that, I own him my apologies. I know that, in spite of difficulties and disappointments, I still sustain love *from within*. Indeed, although my "romantic love" deteriorated through and with objectifications, I still sustain it within the "self." While we no longer meet (or speak), I have learned (seen in pictures, actually) that he has found his way to new romantic love—something that I have tried to do, too—, and I am happy that that is the case, for we all deserve to be cared for as loving (queer) individuals in the course of running. I truly wish him nothing more than love itself. He is truly a beautiful, dear one. I love him, or perhaps the love-embracing idea of him which I have/had, and which lingers, bringing me back to the "in-between," and to the umbrella which I once held for him—an idea which constitutes my current situatedness of longing, my running course of becoming.

And so, at this current moment, as I run this course of a complicated conversation feeling more or less anew, "romantic love" teaches me to unfold, to (re)construct my "self" in the face of empty-handedness, especially in moments of solitude, and to become a more relational person for my own relational "self"—a betterment that I hope to demonstrate in progressive "in-between" moments of my life with beloved (queer) others, too.

4.5 Labor love

In a world of (neo)liberal becomings, loving one's labor can become a complicated conversation.

I was always quite attuned to my work, but confronting the deterioration of "romantic love" in the course of running, and feeling great responsibilities to deliver change as I thought about the collective, this work seemed more and more important to me: "labor love" began to constitute *the* facet of my becoming.

I enjoyed spending my days immersed in readings and writings. I liked to think that my work could contribute to a larger project. I would say that I cared for and about those who worked with me, too. But labor love must have its limits, I heard, sometime later, when my labor love seemed to fault: we have to live and to love the other many facets of becoming(s), and to be "professional" in the course of running, too.

Unlike the proposition set by Samuel D. Rocha (2020) that *curriculum vitae* can be read as a "curriculum of life" (p. 28), I was called to create objectified divisions in the course, including divisions between my "curriculum vitae"—which entailed all my chronological accomplishments and qualifications, and labor obligations—and my "curriculum-as-lived"—which would ironically constitute the experiences lived *outside* of the world of work. *Could life be constitutive of work?* I reluctantly heard this call for a "no" space for the "in-betweens": for a "no" connection between "life" and "work," for the relegation and dismissal of the love that can forge the two.

Now that I think regressively and critically about my own relationship with labor, I am drawn to divergencies and convergencies and to groups and individuals. As I have espoused in CWSJL, based on the work of several curricularists, I now realize that while we can labor in solitude, the work is (or needs to be) intrinsically and increasingly relational and autobiographical, rather than just institutional—a juxtaposition that may also call for novel institutional arrangements.

The world is constantly changing as we adopt and (un)willingly incorporate new technologies in the field of education (and beyond). Most recently, Pinar (2022) employed the method of *currere* to understand technology as con(text) in curriculum work. Just as in previous times, such as the industrial revolution of the 1760 onwards, our relationship with work has changed as a result of our interactions with new objects—such as Artificial Intelligence—, and, consequently, with our own relational "selves." For example, during these "novel" complex times, micro-credentials have sustained faulty theories of change wherein competence discourses and the not-so-inclusive practices of the "gig economy" are promulgated (see Wheelahan & Moodie, 2021)—thus fostering circuits of precariousness that trespass the lines of the so-called "world of work" to constitute our situatedness of becoming.

In this changing world of complex becoming(s), I have attempted to labor in solitude and with others. In solitude, I faced criticisms. You see, I long to be and to labor *with* others while enjoying moments of solitude, attempting to break and (yet) to forge the lines that divide "the personal" from "the professional." When I use the word 'professional' to qualify the matter of relationships—this strange word that attempts to locate my 'self' either in the realms of the 'public' *or* the 'private'—, I feel that I distance my "self" from the alterity that resides in "the other side." Rather than building, sustaining, and crossing the bridge, I locate myself farther from the proximity I value. In other words, I do not know to what extent "the professional" can convey the nexus which I aspire to build in curriculum work (and beyond). I believe that love becomes wanting once we situate our "selves" within the hierarchical and competitive structures of this increasingly professional—rather than relational—world.

I have therefore appreciated the word 'personal' to convey my "labor love." But now that I appreciate more personal close relationships—perhaps more than ever before—, I may look way too private. Such privacy may, on the other hand, distance my "self" from the "proximity" which I aspire to build *with* others—another paradox. I have therefore unfolded at this present moment to better comprehend the importance of building, sustaining, and dwelling in close-knit communities where I am able to pay close attention to "the personal," the relational.

Our societies and the world of work have grown to ostracize "the personal" so that we can live more "professionally." The unison permeates the surface, but people continue *to race* the course *of* development to become—and not always *from within*. This has to be one of the many calls of the Post-Reconceptualization era: to study this complex juxtaposition between "the global," the "the local," and the overall "professional" processes that circumscribe our ways of being and becoming in the world. As I study and attempt to forge 'nexus' and 'proximity' within and across con(texts)—as well as within and across their many paradoxical "in-betweenness"—from a fortified nexus of love, I strengthen my love for this complicated labor. I continue to seek the unfolding so that we can forge (and live) more collective, relational, and contextual becoming(s).

Of course, "we are all perfect and (yet) incomplete" (see CWSJL, Chapter 2), and, in this incompleteness, I still have so much to study, to see, to experience, to bifocalize… a kind of "thinking in action" that may support my unfolding to become a more loving and *consciente* person in/for the world. In this world of complicated becomings, I have surely felt the hurdles intrinsic to this hierarchical and competitive course. Indeed, in my relation with my own incompleteness, I might have not seen alterity in unfolding plenitude at all times. Growing up in a world with people who experienced true scarcities, unlearning some kinds of dispositions is hard labor; to envision a world of there-can-be-plenty and a world of care-can-be-given is not always easy. I often feel the *responsibility of representation* on my shoulders for being a former "have-not." More often than not, I urge my "self" to achieve *more* rather than *less* so that others who come before are seen and truly believe that dreams are not just a possibility—but a reality. Conversing with individuals who dwell in similar con(texts), I know that such discourse *and* feelings are constantly shared.

While at Harvard, one of the professors liked to give care to his students by gifting pencils. He advised us to always have a pencil in hand so as to write our thoughts on paper. He cared for and about our "practical" and "intellectual" labor. I had already developed that practice in college, but I did not practice it profusely, and so I gave greater attention to these words. His encouragement helped me associate creative meanings to the object of pencils later on. So, different from the meanings attributed to pencils in places such as Apartheid South Africa—when these objects would be placed in an individuals' hair to evaluate whether or not the subject was "White enough" (da Silva, 2008)—, his pencils spurred both my writing and my thinking, ultimately helping me showcase my laborious labor of love.

Over the years, creative meanings have reverberated through my writing; my "love labor" has unfolded through several personal and collective projects, especially now as I attempt to forge "nexus" and

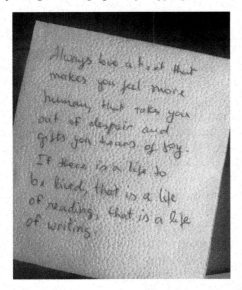

Image 4.2 Written statement about love and curriculum work. Photographed by the author.

"proximity." When I was writing CWSJL, I thought about my relationship with curriculum studies and with the course of running itself. Looking at a napkin which was lying on top of my table, I wrote the following statement (see Image 4.2). I later shared it with my supervisor at the University of British Columbia, as a gift.

I am a curricularist laboring and dwelling in the intersections of theory, policy, and practice. I love this labor and the unfolding, as well as those who run this course with me. And, so, I continue to study, to bifocalize, through reading and writing, this unfolding autobiographical lexis, in order to better understand my relationship with "incompleteness," with "self," and with "alterity"—to advance this vision of curriculum as a collective public moral enterprise in this "nexus moment" (Jales Coutinho, 2022, p. 51), and to fortify this nexus of love, as we go on and on, living and running our contextually complicated lives.

4.6 Converging through and with care: from crises to proliferation

The field of curriculum studies has often been named moribund, troubled by problems of knowledge, relevance, and practicality (e.g. Deng & Twining, 2009; Wheelahan, 2010). But I'd argue that the most profound crisis of curriculum is a crisis of love *and* understanding. Here, I write about convergence and pose questions for our collective dwelling.

As this book suggests, love shares many meanings, and people may attribute a plethora of "objective functions" to it in a world of complex becoming(s). David M. Halperin (2019) once wrote that "love's most important social function nowadays is to promote the acceptability of customary forms of social life" (p. 396). In CWSJL and in this text, I support the idea that the nexus of love—love, hospitality, and solidarity—must be fortified, and that love can eradicate vulnerabilities and suffering in the course of development. When one loves, one cares deeply and intentionally for/about dignity, wellbeing, and flourishing—entailing both short- and long-term dedication to self and alterity's wellbeing, including the unfolding that might happen after one's lifetime. As indicated by Kamani (2021), we are "spiritual beings having a human experience" (p. 1). The hard labor associated with Post-Reconceptualization concerns the coalescence of our subjectivities as we run this course of complicated conversations to forge a nexus of love in our becoming. Convergence is pivotal for undertaking a *collective* project, one where we become subjects from/of/for/through love.

Although meanings and approaches to love may differ and although love may because constrained by structures and power, we should not err in believing that "care" does not constitute our lived experiences in the world. Care is love, however transfigured it becomes within hierarchies of power. *Is there an essence in love?* Or, as Halperin (2019) alludes to, a "standardization" of it? (p. 398). When I write about divergences, I am also drawn to qualifications. As we diverge, we may end up qualifying the love we feel for others. We may employ in our autobiographical lexis words such as "parental love," "romantic love," and "queer love." These qualifications characterize these various relationships which are mostly grounded on social expectations and on particularities. For example, when I experienced "queer love" holding an umbrella, that care was common and yet different to other moments of care which I experienced in other queer relationships. Yet, even within that difference, within that lingering, there was convergence through moments of care/giving. As we "return to love," one can argue that a "standardization of love" is taking place in curriculum studies. However, care is contextual, relational, and symbiotic, culminating in and from conversation and understanding.

Because of this hierarchical and antagonistic course, returning to love in convergence constitutes the most profound crises of curriculum. After all, people do not always find themselves in a situation where they can converge, trapped in a paradoxical course *of* development whose only viable becoming is attrition, long-term conflict, and protectionism, that is, the creation and consolidation of divergence—firm boundaries that do not intersect. For example, in CWSJL, I did not consider the ways through which broken trust and trauma can directly affect *hospitality* in the course of development, and how a lack of understanding of one's circumstances of becoming might facilitate the hope of one finding humanity. Back then, I mentioned that people in their most vulnerable condition, "having few or no capabilities to offer anything of immediate return in exchange, [would] only hope that their humanity find others' as they run the course of their lives" (Jales Coutinho, 2022, p. 44). Notwithstanding, as people become more *consciente* of the oppression and injustices they experience/have experienced and of their trauma, such hope might be erased/replaced because one may reckon that there is no more hope left in humanity. Hence, in meeting "the other" while seeking refuge in a state of trauma, one might just expect to find a place of "survival" where one can linger in one's own solitude and close circle—a predicament which might have direct implications for how s/he might go about entering in conversations, trusting/sharing, and living *with* others. The Post-Reconceptualist crises of curriculum is individual, collective, and international.

In the course of development, nation-states have arisen in the global scene (Wimmer & Feinstein, 2010), and, in international relations, the nation-state constitutes an entity in itself which seeks its own "survival" in a self-help system (realism) (Brown & Ainley, 2009). Teaching history, the nation will certainly attempt to circulate its history in curriculum con(texts) to maintain and boost its legitimacy, status, and recognition. The children can absorb this history as their own becoming, at times placing it above other con(texts), forging the phenomena which we usually call nationalism, which is essential for the survival of the nation-state. But would it be possible for nation-states to teach history as the course of running *in development* (the course in which humans set and conquered frontiers, often through colonization), emphasizing how we came from a position of love and hospitality to one of solidarity, galvanizing conversations concerning how to return to a place of love in such a course? What would this mean for nation-states? Can we envision/imagine another form of global governance or are we truly caught up in this system?

In other words, the nation-state works in a paradox, having to promote its own histories while rooting for cosmopolitanism in order to promote "peace" and *protect* its own existence in a "self-help" international system, hoping to establish power balances with other actors for a mutually constitutive existence. Not surprisingly, the international system has primarily focused on order and security, and then wellbeing (Rapley, 2007); however, if we promote love as the means and ends of development, focusing instead on dignity, wellbeing, and flourishing (love), what would this mean to the international system and to global governance? Once again, we might have some lessons to learn from Indigenous scholars who have been paving the way in re-imagining new systems of governance (e.g. DavidSuzukiFDN, 2021).

We certainly live in a paradoxical world where individuals are "remind[ed]" of their own power [to] give direction into how to end war" (Gibbs, 2021, p. 188) *and* to promote 'just' war. Such power is often garnered through the accumulation of capital and technologies, as well as through the maintenance of status and prestige, articulated through tactics of war and/or diplomacy, aiming at shifts of power, and, theoretically, balance as peace. Indeed, *power shifting* constitutes the lexis of our current development, rather than *power sharing*. After all, trusting and loving others have been conceived as a dangerous enterprise in the course *of* development. But while we can "live" in a world without trust (and only with laws which set both a 'common' framework of understanding on legality *and* implicit messages regarding shared mistrust) and decaying love, trust (not laws) is paramount for the unfolding of genuine hospitality and for love itself to flourish.

If we aspire to overcome the crises as we navigate within and across our subjectivities and structures to produce work that is "aesthetically cohesive, new, different, and yet common" (Jales Coutinho, 2022, p. 51), I contend that curricularists ought to center care/giving in our propositions. Our ways of giving love, of caring for and about others, relationally and contextually, from the standpoint of love itself, that constitutes fortified love. Once again, love is not "standard." It intersects, converging, while our subjectivities push the boundaries of our work outwards, towards divergence, which is expected—after all, curriculum is a "complicated conversation" (Pinar, 2019). But love makes "the whole" of the curriculum possible through "creative transformations" (Doll & Jung, 2016, p. xii). It is caregiving—this kind of love-as-genesis which gives care to forge something 'aesthetically coherent, new, different, and yet common,' even through and in moments of despair—that can forge our path for a Post-Reconceptualization that is collective, public, and moral.

The fortification of love in curriculum, as both an idea and an action, is paramount not only to our "survival," but to relationality and flourishing, that is, to new becomings. Converging in divergence is hard labor. Indeed, as we run and dwell, bifocalizing the "self," much is demanded from us (see, for example, "Confronting fears," Chapter 2 in CWSJL). But persistence is needed in this historical juncture. To converge in a hierarchical, not-so-kind world of becoming(s) aiming to imagine and actualize the course otherwise with others is an autobiographical labor of love.

References

Barlas, A. (2013). Uncrossed bridges: Islam, feminism and secular democracy. *Philosophy & Social Criticism, 39*(4–5), 417–425. https://doi.org/10.1177/019 1453713477346

Brooks, M. C., & Mutohar, A. (2018). Islamic school leadership: A conceptual framework. *Journal of Educational Administration and History, 50*(2), 54–68. https://doi.org/10.1080/00220620.2018.1426558

Brown, C., & Ainley, K. (2009). *Understanding international relations*. Palgrave Macmillan.

da Silva, T. S. (2008). Redeeming self: The business of Whiteness in post-apartheid South African writing. In A. Moreton-Robinso, M. Cayse, & F. Nicoll (Eds.), *Transnational whiteness matters: myth understanding* (pp. 3–18). Lexington Books.

DavidSuzukiFDN. (2021). *Webinar: Land governance: Towards a more just future — Understanding the 'land back' movement*. YouTube. Retrieved October 8, 2022, from https://www.youtube.com/watch?v=oKnyMjQGO5s

Deng, F., & Twining, W. (2009). *Human rights: Southern voices*. Cambridge University Press.

Doll, W., & Jung, J.-H. (2016). *The concept of care in curriculum studies: Juxtaposing currere and Hakbeolism* (pp. xi–xiii). Routledge.

Duderija, A. (2020). Contemporary Muslim male reformist thought and gender equality affirmative interpretations of Islam. *Feminist Theology, 28*(2), 161–181. https://doi.org/10.1177/0966735019886076

Esposito, J. L. (2011). *What everyone needs to know about islam* (2nd ed.). Oxford University Press.

Gibbs, B. (2021). "So my grandfather's two tours meant nothing?": Students struggle with the weight and responsibility of war. *Journal of Curriculum and Pedagogy, 19*(3), 187–210. https://doi.org/10.1080/15505170.2020.1869123

Halperin, D. M. (2019). Queer love. *Critical Inquiry, 45*(2), 396–419. https://doi.org/10.1086/700993

Independent. (2019). *Aoc asks pharma CEO why $2,000 HIV drug costs just $8 in Australia: 'People are dying for no reason.' The Independent*. Digital News and Media. Retrieved March 25, 2022, from https://www.independent.co.uk/news/world/americas/us-politics/aoc-hiv-drug-cost-us-australia-ceo-gilead-video-a8919316.html

Jales Coutinho, A. M. (2022). *Curriculum work and social justice leadership in a post-reconceptualist era: Attaining critical consciousness and learning to become* (1st ed.). Routledge. https://doi.org/10.4324/9781003188629

Kamani, F. (2021). The serendipity of surrender. *Holistic Education Review*, *1*(2), 1–4.

Kottak, C. P. (2019). *Mirror for humanity: A concise introduction to cultural anthropology*. McGraw-Hill Education.

Ladson-Billings, G. (2006). From the achievement gap to the education debt: Understanding achievement in U.S. Schools. *Educational Researcher*, *35*(7), 3–12. https://doi.org/10.3102/0013189x035007003

Mullett, M. A. (2015). *Martin Luther* (2nd ed.). Routledge.

Niyozov, S. (2010). Teachers and teaching Islam and Muslims in pluralistic societies: Claims, misunderstandings, and responses. *Journal of International Migration and Integration/Revue De L'integration Et De La Migration Internationale*, *11*(1), 23–40. https://doi.org/10.1007/s12134-009-0123-y

Noddings, N. (2008). Spirituality and religion in public schooling. *Teachers College Record*, *110*(13), 185–195. https://doi.org/10.1177/016146810811001315

Patrick, M. L. (2015). A call for more religious education in the secondary social studies curriculum of Western Canadian provinces. *Curriculum Inquiry*, *45*(2), 154–175. https://doi.org/10.1080/03626784.2015.1011043

Pinar, W. F. (2019). *What is curriculum theory?*. Routledge.

Pinar, W. F. (2022). *A praxis of presence in curriculum theory: Advancing currere against cultural crises in education* (1st ed.). Routledge. https://doi.org/10.4324/9781003212348

Rapley, J. (2007). *Understanding development: Theory and practice in the third world*. Lynne Rienner Publishers.

Rocha, S. D. (2020). *The syllabus as curriculum: A reconceptualist approach* (1st ed.). Routledge. https://doi.org/10.4324/9780429027901

Rowley, M. P., & Wild-Wood, E. (2017). Religion, hermeneutics and violence: An introduction. *Transformation: An International Journal of Holistic Mission Studies*, *34*(2), 77–90. https://doi.org/10.1177/0265378816659997

Stafford, J. (2016). Looking to the past and moving to the future: A catholic high school religious curriculum for the 21st century. *Historia De La Educación*, *35*, 105. https://doi.org/10.14201/hedu201635105121

Twining, W. (Ed.). (2009). *Human rights: Southern voices – Francis Deng, Abdullahi An-Na'im, Yash Ghai, and Upendra Baxi*. Cambridge University Press.

Wheelahan, L. (2010). *Why knowledge matters in curriculum*. Taylor and Francis.

Wheelahan, L., & Moodie, G. (2021). Gig qualifications for he gig economy: Micro-credentials and the 'Hungry Mile'. *Higher Education*. https://doi.org/10.1007/s10734-021-00742-3

Wimmer, A., & Feinstein, Y. (2010). The rise of the nation-state across the world, 1816 to 2001. *American Sociological Review*, *75*(5), 764–790. https://doi.org/10.1177/0003122410382639

World Bank. (2015). *World Bank Development Report 2015: Mind, society, and behaviour*. World Bank. https://doi.1596/978-1-4648-0342-0. License: Creative Commons Attribution CC BY 3.0 IGO.

5 Love and justice in evaluations in societies and in schools

Love and justice constitute two pivotal words of/for a social justice lexicon. I began to employ these more frequently in my autobiographical vernacular when I started to study the field of law in the United States and Japan, and later the field of curriculum studies in Canada. Justice and its theories were so complicated, and yet so interesting and appealing. Now that I think more deeply about love and justice, I also take stock of the ways through which these are employed in the field of education and curriculum, and how evaluations—a key object of governmentality—can mediate, dissect, and/or deconstruct love in an antagonistic, agonistic, and competitive world of becomings, especially in the democratic institutions that are meant to guarantee and foster order, security, and wellbeing, including schools.

If we think critically about "evaluations" and "assessments" as objects of governmentality, they are not only employed in the field of education as a means to examine how individuals are progressing in each "discipline," but also used as an object within other democratic institutions. For example, when a prosecutor brings forth a case to a judge, s/he evaluates the merits of the case in order to issue his/her understanding of it, using codes and precedents to determine what is just and fair according to the legal tradition in place (see, for example, Merryman & Pérez-Perdomo, 2007). Likewise, when a teacher employs a summative evaluation, she might also perceive that object as the sole determinant of students' failure or success, a dichotomy that may place these individuals and their subjectivities in fixed limbos of destitution.

Because educational systems are usually structured into a tripod of policies—curriculum, teaching professional development, and assessment— and because criticism against evaluations are commonplace in education, often contradicting the very concept of care in curriculum work, I dedicate this chapter to this topic. I contend that the study of

DOI: 10.4324/9781003359968-5

evaluations, constitutive of educational and legal systems, is pivotal for curriculum and for the unfolding of autobiography. After all, the object of evaluation is a part of our institutional con(text), too. Indeed, as suggested in previous chapters, policies and laws operationalize power and shape experience, including our experience with care in the world. As pointed out by Steve Vago (2009), as societies turned into more complex organisms, laws became a part of the institutional con(text) of development, which demanded the codification of norms and expectations for social cohesion. As a context, we can study laws as part of our autobiographies and reflect how such con(text) can be altered so that love can be less negotiated.

I dwell in and run this course of a complicated conversation, theorizing the role that "evaluations" may enjoy in a Post-Reconceptualist era of curriculum work as a collective public moral enterprise. I invite curricularists to seek contexts (including contexts that may not have yet been imagined or materialized) and to employ their "social imagination" (Greene, 1995) to develop a critical and (yet) creative stand on "evaluations" as we move towards a progression, a place and moment in time where love can be less negotiated in our daily encounters.

In this text, I envision a world where "caregiving," relational and contextual "autobiographical understandings," and "actualization" constitute the epicentre of curriculum-as-plan. I follow Jung's (2016) reasoning and employ the word "actualization" (p. 35) together with "self-actualization"—in lieu of "evaluations" and "self-evaluations"—to convey new meanings for "assessments" in a Post-Reconceptualist era of curriculum studies. I argue that "actualization" does not convey the "attainment" and "evaluation" of knowledge and skills, but rather the relational and contextual *realization* on the part of the subject of his/her unfolding in the course of development.

These are moments of critical agency, moments in which subjects *mobilize academic knowledge* in their "academic study" (Pinar, 2011, p. xiii), from a fortified nexus of love, threading their subjectivities to ultimately transform their autobiographical lexis, ways of knowing/being, as well as situatedness of becoming. I contend that as individuals "become temporal" (Pinar, 2019, p. 4) and historical, running and dwelling in the course of running, seeking contexts, crossing bridges—ultimately (i) disrupting single thoughts, (ii) denominating circuits of privilege and oppression, and (iii) promoting relational and contextual autobiographical understandings (see Jales Coutinho, 2022, p. 15)—they become "actualized." As I hope to demonstrate in this text, unfolding and actualization are interconnected, juxtaposing each other in a world of/for new becoming(s).

Because we have been immersed in social milieus that employ "evaluations" of all kinds, it can be hard to imagine "life otherwise." Thus, to galvanize thinking and action, I share the following questions before delineating Post-Reconceptualist theories and arguments about (self-)actualization (and love) in curriculum work. I call upon curricularists to run and dwell on these questions before proceeding. I also remind curricularists that questions pertaining to curriculum are not disconnected from questions about the structures of societies and, consequently, from the meanings we attribute to care(work). After all, curriculum policies are often an expression of the societies that craft them, and vice versa:

(i) *Is it possible to envision and to actualize lived experiences free of 'assessments' in schools when other democratic institutions employ such mechanisms to administer 'justice' and, in a way, to sustain democracy?*

(ii) *Which kind of society/social structures/institutions would be able to deliver 'justice' without the employment of assessments? Would these societies maintain and administer order, security, and wellbeing for all—the current tripod of development? Or would these societies be able to proliferate (just) love instead, making vulnerabilities a myth?*

(iii) *If we perceive an "evaluation" as an object, can we attribute other meanings to it in order to turn it into 'a subject' of love for the educational con(text) rather than a mere instrument/object of governmentality?*

In the paragraphs and the pages that follow, I describe how "evaluations" constitute our situatedness of becoming in the post-modern, post-human world. I emphasize the role that each play in legal and educational systems worldwide. First, I briefly describe how "legal" and "educational" assessments have been created in the course of development, each emphasizing the role of evaluations, and how they are connected to the global phenomena of generalizations (subsection 5.1). Second, I write about legal systems and differentiate some of the facets pertaining to the civil and common law traditions, shedding light on how the courts evaluate cases in each tradition in the search for "truth" as they attempt to administer/deliver justice and promote reconciliation (subsection 5.2). I intersect and juxtapose the meanings that circulate the court with those of the curriculum and the classrooms to exemplify how educational caregivers can also develop the tendency to judge people, situations, and institutions using hard, objective criteria whilst (i) employing methods of comparisons and (ii) attributing meanings to subjects, the classroom, and the school (curriculum) (subsection 5.3).

The juxtapositions that I offer in these subsections (subsections 5.2 and 5.3) are pivotal. As I have alluded, the meanings that circulate the court and the classroom can be quite analogous. Indeed, I argue that mode of "judgementality," which also sustain our governmentality, permeates the fabric of democratic institutions of all kinds, including schools. In CWSJL, I gave an account of the Foucauldian concept of "governmentality" and unfolded the concept of "subjectivementality" to describe a mentality which:

> Embraces curriculum-as-lived and its qualitative ways of knowing as a valid form of knowledge for decision making; a mentality that seeks to understand the complex, subjective, and intricate ways in which different people live their lives, experience phenomena in schools (and beyond), and respond to privilege and oppression in their daily encounters with the (un)known; and a mentality that seeks to center love and justice as the means and ends of development.
> (Jales Coutinho, 2022, p. 130)

In this book, I coin another term—the term "judgementality"—to describe moments in which individuals judge self, alterity, situations, and institutions using hard, objective criteria whilst employing methods of comparisons. Such mentality severs relationships, for people become inclined to compare and rank objects and objectified subjects rather than relate with them, from a nexus of love. As I hope to demonstrate, judgementality and governmentality are intrinsically connected. In this text, I underscore how we can *collectively* approach "actualization" in schools, shifting from modes of "governmentality" and "judgementality" to "subjectivementality" in our encounters with alterity—including educators and students— nature, and the cosmos, in the larger educational polity.

In this text, I argue that teachers may be able to support students in the *unfolding* and in their *actualization* by sharing questions and insights through a dialectical approach. Once again, I contend that the unfolding, which is tantamount to "learning to become," cannot be "evaluated," only *actualized*. In order to shed light on questions pertaining to actualization, I employ the autobiographical con(text) in the final section of this chapter to provide additional insights for educators and policymakers (Subsection 5.4). Here, I argue that while the standardization of "curriculum-as-plan" may be able to support certain "theories of change" in education (Jales Coutinho, 2021), the unfolding will unlikely be standardized. I theorize that while "external evaluations" may support the subject during initial processes of actualization, there might be a moment in the unfolding—a moment where the subject attains greater levels of *conscientização*, departing from a fortified nexus of love to forge relational *and* contextual autobiographical understandings *with* relational and beloved others—wherein "external evaluations" become obsolete in the course *of* development, in our futurity.

5.1 Evaluations and generalizations

Running and dwelling are pivotal undertakings in/for curriculum work. This nexus can position the collective in a better place to see (and actualize) "life otherwise." Life can surely be a kind of a contentious, unfolding phenomena—studying it can be arduous, too. But as we face many bridge(s) in our lives, running and dwelling, we are also invited to think beyond the personal and the relational to envision the collective anew. As I have alluded to in CWSJL, I depart from the premise that individuals can enact their "critical agencies" (Jales Coutinho, 2022, p. 4) in the world, that societies and their institutions are not the only forces that can shape the course of development, for the individual can generate meanings, produce and employ discourses, theories, and practices that can ultimately transform the course, too.

In CWSJL, I have also pointed out to some of the personal and collective dilemmas that curricularists face when they conduct research in the course of running (see Chapter 4, "A Lingering Note"). Indeed, as we think about the collective—the curriculum as a collective public moral enterprise—we confront several dilemmas. Such dilemmas permeate not only the world of schooling, but also the fabric of other institutions which have been built to protect and safeguard rights and freedoms in our (neo)liberal democracies. In this subsection, I revisit the dilemma of generalizations, but at this time making a direct link with "evaluations"—in the legal world and in the world of schooling. I later juxtapose meanings and provide more details about each to theorize about "actualization" in Post-Reconceptualization.

In the study of philosophy, legal practitioners are called upon to think relentlessly about the rule of law. I argue that, as curricularists, we have to set our minds to these questions too if we are to imagine and theorize a world where love is proliferated, and then find ways to forge nexus, to *actualize* such a world in schools (and beyond)—be it through the design of curriculum/educational policies, public health policies in schools etc. In the world of governmentality, curriculum can be theorized as "a disciplinary technique through which individuals embody institutional practices and values that seek to create compliant, governable populations habituated to prevailing modes of social, political, and economic organization" (Burns, 2018, p. vii). Compliance is not tantamount to relational and contextual caregiving, however. Here, the Post-Reconceptualist curriculum question reverberates: *Which condition(s) and arrangement(s) can allow for / facilitate the proliferation of love in our lives and in our work?*

Now, think about a society where no laws govern the relationships among individuals—or a place where laws are not obeyed— where people are able to do as they wish, such as in the allegory of *the Lord of the Flies* (Golding, 2018). Chaos and death could be one of the likely outcomes. In this scenario, order would need to be maintained, especially if people did not trust and relate with one another. A power would eventually rise and set norms so that people could interact with one another and eschew from the "state of nature"—a state which can comparable to that of endemic corruption (Morigiwa, 2015). This power would ultimately find a way to maintain "balance" with other aspiring powers in the course *of* development. In order to govern these relationships, a legal system could be set in place, too. But to establish such a system, one would need to think about "the whole," the collective, and make generalizations.

The legal scholar Lon Fuller (2010) provides interest insights into this quandary. He lists eight ways through which one can fail to make law. One of the first questions raised concerns the "powers of generalization" (Fuller, 2010, p. 27). The person in charge of creating codes has to be able to make even the simplest generalizations from reason if s/he is to devote his/her time and labor to contribute to this enterprise. As suggested by Fuller (2010), even if someone opted to evaluate and rule cases, ultimately drawing "patterns" to provide reasons for his/her adjudications, this would require great skill, technology, and memory so as to avoid confusion and misleads—clarity and predictability constitute some of the conditions to sustain the rule of law in a polity. In a nutshell, "lessons in generalization" (Fuller, 2010, p. 28) are key if one aspires to make law and sustain a legal system to serve the entire population and to avoid the "state of nature"—a state where order, security, and wellbeing are not attained.

These assumptions and lessons have given rise to a "contract theory" in political science, a theory that espouses that "the sovereign [is] not appointed through God, but that his/her position [is] legitimated through a fictitious social contract (...) whereby unrestrained individual power enjoyed in the 'state of nature' is surrendered to the state in return for political order" (Morigiwa et al., 2013, p. 8). In today's world, the judicial/legal system is responsible to administer and deliver justice. The courts evaluate cases on an ongoing basis as they receive written statements and conduct hearings. In the process, they determine which competing theories (including those provided by the specialists) can be used in the provision of the 'best' reasons to settle (at least provisionally) complicated cases/conversations. Of course, the public expects judges to maintain a watchful eye on their own conduct too, so as to not corrupt the system which is enshrined to safeguard the rights of the citizenry.

In CWSJL, I argued that such "lessons in generalization" have become a major turnabout in the course of development, especially with the aid of statistical theory, a "technology" which has allowed managers of the public sphere to provide reasons to design and implement policies at scale—certainly a necessary endeavour considering the rise of the human population and the institutionalization of human rights discourses. In the world of school systems, statistical theory—most specifically, classical test theory (CTT) and item response theory (IRT)—has allowed educational leaders and scholars to employ exams to a large number of individuals (Sousa & Braga, 2020). Originated in the apogee of eugenic thinking, in the first decades of the twentieth century, CTT has made it possible to control and predict measurement "error" in exams. Through CTT, statisticians have been able to measure the difference between the "true score" (the unobservable score that represents the true ability of the individual) and the "empirical one" (the observable one), which is the obtained score of an individual in an evaluation instrument (Sousa & Braga, 2020). Item response theory (IRT) is considered a more robust model because, compared to CTT, the assumptions that underline the framework do not fit easily with the data (Hambleton & Jones, 1993). IRT has contributed to this enterprise by making the comparability of individual scores from the same population a possibility (Sousa & Braga, 2020). These theories have undoubtedly supported policymakers in the management of educational systems at national, state, and municipal levels.

As one can see, similar to courts, schools also employ evaluations to manage/control a burgeoning and complex system that attempts to safeguard the rights of *all* populations under constitutional, democratic tenets. Lawmakers and certain courts deliberate about specific cases, having to reach some level of generalization to deliver their reasoning and to serve the public. At the same time, schools employ examinations to evaluate whether students are attaining the desired levels of learning, and hence reaching personal and collective/public aspirations. However, puzzling as this may sound, generalizations and predictability seem to be in service of the public as the world faces a burgeoning rise in populational densities and confronts "exogenous shocks" in the course of development—shocks such as the Covid-19 pandemic and the climate crisis which may look "exogenous," but which are (very) *relational* to our own unfolding and presence on the planet.

Indeed, schools are a part of a large institutional arrangement that employs "disciplinary tactics" (Burns, 2018, p. 3) to control the means and ends of "development." Evaluations produce data about the individual who is then placed under a curve, together with those who participate in the evaluation enterprise, to provide information about that same population. In schools, evaluations are employed to verify whether students are progressing satisfactorily in each discipline and at each educational stage (Green, 1980)—so that they are able to "become" more active, responsible, productive citizens of the polity and fulfill the democratic premises of equality and opportunity: "if we employ exams to evaluate students, we will be able to support and help them achieve the adequate levels of learning in mathematics, languages, etc." This is usually *the* theory of change associated with exams in the world of educational policymaking: exams (monitoring) are (is) necessary if we are to (realistically) deliver some form of (quantifiable) change in the world. But, of course, this is just *one* of the myriad of meanings that students, educators, and policymakers *can* attribute to the object of "evaluation." Embedded in the theory is the presumption that exams can support *achievement*, but achievement is often enacted *through competition*—and unprincipled competition often becomes the nadir of democratic tenets.

In a nutshell, evaluations allow for generalizations—and generalizations are seemingly connected to "the collective." From the outset, evaluations and generalizations are key for the "management" of a burgeoning population, and for the attainment of rights in a not-so-kind-of relational world, too. But evaluations can also allow for harmful generalizations in a (racist, transphobic, chauvinistic, Islamophobic etc. and hierarchical) world of comparative and competitive becomings. Undoubtedly, the creation and employment of evaluations can become a part of an "audit culture" (Burns, 2018, p. 8). They can constitute the nadir of educational experiences of a population who may endure some form of hidden (or not-so-hidden) oppression in the course of schooling. As Samuel D. Rocha (2020) rightly points out:

"the subject, the human person, is also the one who makes objects" (p. 25). Indeed, objects are often created and designed to receive and to distribute weaponized, coercive meanings in a world full of hurt—a world where self and alterity are constantly positioned/perceived as an imminent threat.

The Brazilian educator Cipriano Carlos Luckesi (2011) argues that "science describes and interprets reality, [whereas] evaluations describe and qualify such realities" (p. 171). However, other scholars may argue that evaluations, as objects of governmentality, have been created to *forge* reality. This is why evaluations are so controversial: the population attributes incongruous meanings/theories of change which circulate/constitute the object in the world of schooling—some theories considered/positioned as negative (see, for example, Burns, 2018, pp. 82–87), and some theories considered/positioned as positive (see, for example, OECD, 2013). This is why subjectivementality is pivotal for education and policymaking, too. Subjectivementality is in service of the public, the collective, in as much as (or perhaps even more than) governmentality. After all, people can use their "judgementalities" to call upon students and to provide reasons and justifications for their "failure," ultimately blaming them for the consequences they might face in the course of schooling *and* development. Punishment is often the very outcome of judgementality. Punishment is not in service of education, however. Relationality and contextuality are. From a fortified nexus of love, they allow the subject and the collective to face "self," "alterity," and "history" through the lens of (re)construction—a locus and a nexus for new becomings.

In the pages that follow, I provide more details on the role that evaluations play in legal and educational systems in order to juxtapose meanings and later theorize about "actualization" in a Post-Reconceptualist era of curriculum studies as a collective public moral enterprise.

5.1.1 Evaluations in the world of legal systems

In the field of legal studies, one can classify different systems within two major law traditions—the civil and the common law— each aiming to deliver justice through specific processes, rules, and understandings of the nature and the role of law (Merryman & Pérez-Perdomo, 2007). Originating many centuries ago, when societies experienced great economic and political transformations, these traditions have been "transferred" to several nations through the intertwined processes of colonization and globalization (Joireman, 2004). Germany, France, and Brazil, as well as other nation-states located in Africa,

Asia, and in the Americas have developed their legal systems following civil law tenets. Conversely, nation-states such as the United States and Canada have abided common law ones.

Many differences exist between these two traditions (see Laeuchli, 2007), but perhaps the most relevant is the approach to litigation and arbitration. Whereas the civil law tradition employs an *inquisitive approach*, the common law tradition approaches litigation and arbitration through an *adversarial* process. In both cases, a trial can be perceived as a "search for truth" (Freedman et al., 2010, p. 2). Generally speaking, in the inquisitive approach, the court plays the majority role in collecting evidence. The parties involved in the conflict and their attorneys are then responsible to oversee that work, participate in hearings, and direct the court's attention to specific, cogent queries that can elucidate the case. In other words, in the inquisitive approach, the trial constitutes a continuous process whereby evidence is simultaneously collected and assessed (Freedman et al., 2010).

Conversely, in the adversarial approach, the parties involved in conflict are responsible to collect and present the evidence. They *compete* against each other to present their case as the most compelling before the court. That means that attorneys and parties are encouraged to display evidence as they see fit, which may constitute one of the defects of adversary theory (Freedman et al., 2010)—a strength of "adversary theory," on the other hand, would be to maintain the "impartiality" of the judge who would not provide provisional views for the litigants on settlement, etc. Moreover, attorneys in the adversary system can also prepare testimonies accordingly so that they can contribute to present their case before the court (Freedman et al., 2010). In the search for "truth," one can argue that the systems ought to preserve "the dignity of the individual, even though that may occasionally require significant frustration of [that] search and the will of the state" (Freedman et al., 2010, p. 4).

Legal scholars and practitioners can speak of several dilemmas and raise a myriad of questions as they argue for and/or against a specific approach and theory in the search, maximization, and service of truth and justice. After all, delivering justice and safeguarding the rule of law while caring for and about the entire population in a "hierarchical" and "competitive" world of "scarce" resources can be a complicated conversation, too. In the world we live in, people constantly delineate the contours of "the frontiers" (Jales Coutinho, 2022, p. 64) with the support of legal systems so that they can stand—rather than *live together with*—one another. However, whether people are able to sustain and proliferate love *from within* in either approach is open to question: relationality may be greatly severed when people reach the down point of turning/positioning alterity and different parties into/as "enemies" prior to and during a trial. Once that position becomes psychologically fixed, replicated over the generations—especially when parties perceive themselves to be "acting defensively rather than deliberately [in the] initiation of a [conflict]" (Brown & Ainley, 2009, p. 9), be it within the realm of international relations or not—it becomes (quite) difficult to reverse such a mindset (Bar-Tal, 2000).

Because of the conflicting nature attributed to the achievement of 'justice' in today's societies—commonly attained via *non-relational, unloving approaches* such as litigation—the legal profession is not commonly perceived as "caregiving." Contrary to professions such as teaching and nursing, the public tends to view attorneys and the whole of the legal arena as an untrusting and benighted enterprise (Freedman et al., 2010). Indeed, legal systems (can) change the transformative, healing role associated with apology and reconciliation—which are also key for closure and new becoming(s)—at times severing and/or commodifying these (see, for example, Taft, 2000; Wolff & Braman, 1999). In a nutshell, to "judge" cases and to attain "the truth" is undoubtedly another type of hard labor, especially when people are not willing/able to think and to act *relationally*, from a fortified nexus of love, to ameliorate conflicting relationships in an agonistic, antagonistic, and competitive world of (a/historical) becomings.

Of course, legal systems are not immutable; they can be sensitive to the unfolding and to the course *of* development. I reckon that the searching/seeking of hard and intractable 'truths' through "evaluations" has transformed individuals and perhaps whole collectives, as well as the institutions that continue to seek such truths through various methods to deliver/achieve 'justice'. For example, I invite curricularists to study the changes in the "landscape of difference" (Soudien, 2010, p. 25) in South Africa and in Canada as a result of the work conducted by their Truth and Reconciliation Commissions (TRCs). While coloniality may still constitute the fabric of these societies, shaping the lived experiences of individuals as they navigate a myriad of paradoxes and complexities (see Stein et al., 2022), their legal systems and educational institutions *have* embraced calls for truth *and* reconciliation. At the discourse level and in some practical instances, approaches to reconciliation have been implemented to promote "decolonial indigenization" (Côté et al., 2021)—and these efforts ought to be studied continuously through "talking with" so that the *collective* can have a better understanding of how reconciliation can be achieved and which efforts are most effective in leveraging *conscientização* (critical consciousness).

Second, I call upon curricularists to acknowledge the changes in the technological methods employed by institutions in the search of/for truth in a "post-human" world (see, for example, Roth, 2017)—a world where the "death of the subject" (Pinar, 2019, pp. 81–85) has been constantly claimed, and not only within classrooms. As we can see, the changes and struggles in the course of development shape institutions (e.g. educational and legal), and the institutions seek approaches to shape their unfolding (which might include the search for truth) according to a myriad of views/mentalities (e.g. humanistic and technocentric) in this course, which in turn contribute to changes in the course *of* development itself—an iterative process. Here, it is important to note that legal systems, just like the school curriculum, are bond to take "turns" throughout the course *of* development, to engage in this iterative process of "change."

For example, whereas judges in the civil law tradition may rely heavily on status to determine where litigants and plaintiffs are positioned within "the frontiers," the common law tradition employs prior rulings (precedent) as a key lever of/for justice. As such, scholars have argued that legal systems pertaining to the common law tradition are more malleable than the civil law ones. However, as Merryman and Pérez-Perdomo (2007) testify, such claims underestimate the influences and transformations that each have upon the other. For example, both legal traditions have embedded the practice of "judicial review," thus enabling judges to rule that certain statutes are unconstitutional, thus diminishing the "exaggerated emphasis on legislative autonomy" and its role as "the sole judge of the legality" (Merryman & Pérez-Perdomo, 2007).

Legality and governmentality are interlinked and increasingly connected to curriculum and teaching—and to forms of judgementality. In contexts where inter- and intra-group conflicts have shaped the course of lives and collective memories, such connection becomes conspicuously evident and a sight for ongoing study. For example, in Apartheid South Africa, lawmaking and governmentality instituted racial classification according to "biological" and "social standing factors," shaping the course of schooling and curricula (Pinar, 2010) whilst forging different lived experiences of becoming for "White," "Coloured," and "Native" South Africans (Posel, 2001). In the Republic of Rwanda, where the lives of over 800,000 Tutsis and moderate Hutus were reaped in 1994, a new kind of governmentality attempted to erase the social constructed lines that divided these groups (Zorbas, 2004). Initially unable to deal with the "legacy of genocide," the country turned to the international community to launch the United Nations International Criminal Tribunal for Rwanda—most precisely the United Nations Security Council, which issued resolution 955 of November 8, 1994 (United Nations, 1994)—and to redesign the curriculum-as-plan, ultimately employing an educational framework similar to the post-Holocaust in Germany (See Davidson, 2018).

In schools, when students engage in behaviour that are deemed inappropriate, teachers often call upon the principals to intervene and, at times, engage in complicated conversations with caregivers from home. Applying and upholding school policies, leadership may be inclined, depending on how they employ their mentalities, to suspend students without studying the multiple con(texts) that may have lead students to act in specific ways—suspensions which may place extremely vulnerable populations in further disadvantage, including in terms of learning. In the world of schooling, judgementalities can severe not only students' tangible, auspicious relationships with schools and educators, but also their relation with *conscientização* and their understanding of and experiences with caregiving. Indeed, judgementalities can sever the very nexus of love that educators ought to fortify; they can also preclude the pursuit of justice in the course of running. After all, if individual blaming constitutes the course of schooling, individuals will feel likely less inclined to:

(i) Seek relational and contextual autobiographical encounters/meanings to constitute the unfolding;
(ii) Acknowledge and face their own mistakes and incompleteness in their course of running; and
(iii) Walk the path towards subject (re)construction and reconciliation with "self," "alterity," "nature," and the "cosmos."

When we collectively employ a mindset of judgementality to judge people, ascribing perceived mistakes to people's senseless "nature," we may end up precluding the (re)constructive "nature of education." If there is an *essence* in education, subject (re)construction truly constitutes it. While legal systems may stand in today's convoluted societies to judge complex cases and deliver justice in a hierarchical and competitive world of becoming(s), educational systems may stand strong to help our collectives (re)construct these societies, contributing to this project of curriculum as collective public moral enterprise—from object to subject and to whole collectives, forging new ways of/for becoming, from a fortified nexus of love. The world needs collective healing due to the nature of the antagonistic, agonistic, and competitive course. Education should stand in the face of these antagonisms to transform the course of running, and to make our humanity more human—and paradoxically incomplete—in the course of schooling (and beyond).

5.1.2 Evaluations in the world of school systems

Evaluations are now very intrinsically connected to the course of schooling. At the outset, education does not seem to exist without them. Indeed, in the world of schools, several evaluations comprise the course: from formative to summative and diagnostic evaluations, students and educators are constantly called upon to exam what they have (not) accomplished. Evaluations are signifiers of both internal and external meanings: they convey messages about the quality of learning to stakeholders located outside of school (external communication), and to learners and educators within schools (internal communication)—people who might or might not perceive these objects as a pedagogical component for learning (and unfolding).

The fulfillment of such pedagogical purpose would depend on several factors, including individuals' willingness to use evaluations as catalysts for individual learning, comparisons and/or competition (see Schneider & Hutt, 2013). Moreover, when decision-makers focus on the "(not) accomplished" whilst employing judgementalities, they can easily circulate, perpetuate, and crystalize deficit thinking narratives (Valencia, 1997) about specific populations. After all, evaluations are constituted not only of items, but also of the grading systems associated with these objects, the "key technology of educational bureaucratization" (Schneider & Hutt, 2013, p. 202).

Because evaluations convey important external messages to stakeholders outside schools such as policymakers, "self-evaluations" are not usually treated as an important managerial and pedagogical "tool." If self-evaluations were to be perceived as a key parameter for educational processes in the world of today, policymakers would need to trust that students and the educational community as a whole would have (i) the necessary knowledge and experiences to determine whether they had fulfilled knowledge gaps (e.g. the curriculum standards) and (ii) the expertise/mindset/ethics of care to rightly point out where the unfolding could occur next.

Unfortunately, we do not seem to live in a world of trust and in a world of knowledge mobilization—but rather in a world of fact-checking and route memorization. Indeed, even state policies that address questions pertaining to home schooling in the United States require that parents report back to school systems, and that students perform some form of evaluation to measure their "progress" as mandated by curriculum standards: policymakers are often concerned about "disastrous adventures" that may place the students and educational systems in comparative disadvantage—and their jobs at risk, too.

Ultimately perceived as objects, evaluations and grading systems are pivotal for the sustenance and revival of our governmentalities. Like people, these objects are *not* neutral. They may be positioned as such by decision-makers, but, again, these are objects, and, as such, they circulate meanings. In various cases, people attribute the meanings that they see best fit, meanings that can aid their own narratives about phenomena and alterity. Indeed, there may be cases in which educators might position students and parents as adversaries, or cases in which administrators may position teachers as adversaries, and vice versa. Playing in an "adversary system," this tool of governmentality can become anything but "pedagogical." People may employ them to collect evidence and to reach to a piece of "truth" to support their theories—some of which can be *truly* against human flourishing (think, for example, about the racial supremacist theories that shaped the course of schooling for Jews in Nazi Germany). With these objects, people may ultimately judge alterity—in many cases, students' and educators' capabilities to perform specific tasks— and "read" their lives *out* of con(text).

As previously suggested, in the history of national school systems, evaluations and grading mechanisms have been brought to scale and standardized. Over time, the increased mobility of students influenced policymakers to call upon "greater standardization," that is, "more efficient, standardized, and coherent mechanisms" (Schneider & Hutt, 2013, p. 208) to manage students across borders and to ensure that grades everywhere could share meaning. Today, the approaches employed by individuals and organizations differ in terms of organization and delivery, but they all attempt to convey standardized meanings of educational *achievement* (learning and skills accumulated over the span of specific timeframes such as school years). For example, the European Credit Transfer and Accumulation System (ECTS) has been established to compare academic credits for higher education institutions across Europe. Although there may exist some pitfalls embedded in such evaluation/grading systems, such as gaming and grade inflation, evaluations continue to shape and mediate the lived experiences of becoming in schools.

Recognizing discrepancies in approaches to evaluations at the national level, policymakers have raised the question: *Which evaluational approaches are most effective in improving education quality and learning?* (see, for example, Clarke, 2012). It is important to note that, by asking this and other similar questions, managers and educators are accepting the role of evaluations as a taken-for-granted object in the world of schooling—an object that will continue to constitute our situatedness of becoming "here" and "there," "now" and "then," regardless of changes in con(texts). That is, evaluations are "here" to stay, regardless of whether or not students unfold their *conscientização* to actualize their own learning and becoming in the course of development. They are "here" to stay regardless of one's age, social positioning, and economic status, etc. In a nutshell, evaluations are treated as one of the few mechanisms that can deliver change in 21st century education (see, for example, World Bank Group, 2018).

As we begin to image a future which has not yet materialized, a world of possibilities for new relational and contextual becomings, we may ask our "selves" some pivotal questions in order to question the taken-for-granted processes that constitute our lived experiences of becoming in schools. I am speaking about questions that may ultimately lead us to a "progression" where our educational institutions (and the individuals that comprise them) become better positioned to attain greater levels of *conscientização* and approach justice through our subjectivementalities, from a fortified nexus of love. For example: *Can we reach a moment in human history where evaluations would become obsolete? What could lead us to this moment? Could there be a moment in history where self-evaluations would be praised over external evaluations? Why would this be desirable?*

Attempting to provide some insights that may help us answer some of these questions, I employ the autobiographical con(text) in regressive, progressive, analytical, and synthetical moments, together with bifocalization, to highlight my own experiences with the object of evaluation in the course of running. By doing so, I speak about the role that "actualization" may play in a Post-Reconceptualist era in schools (and beyond). The autobiographical text that follows is an autobiographical narrative about unfolding, actualization, and becoming.

5.2 Actualization in post-reconceptualization: an autobiographical account

Speeding in the corridor, late to get to my first English class, I reached the door and knocked on it. No sound echoed from within. That door, once opened, would transfer my "self" to linger in a new "in-between," in a new kind of reality: one where I would navigate between modes of knowing, achieving, and becoming.

As the narrow space created by the door widened, I saw my classmates in their desks, and the teacher by her table, calling my peers' names, filling the attendance sheet. Afraid of interrupting, I did not utter a word. I entered the classroom and sit in the last row. After the attendance had been completed, the teacher underscored the need for students to excuse themselves before entering the classroom. She encouraged students to say these words, which at the time I did not understand: "Excuse me, may I come in?"

Feeling embarrassed, I thought to myself how difficult that experience would be: I only knew three or four English words at the time, as well as some personal pronouns. Some form of evaluation had already permeated the interactions in that classroom. Later I would understand that that teacher just wished the best for her students. Besides English, she would constantly teach us the very cultural/social capital that would help us navigate a world of etiquette and protocols—a world where judgementality would constitute the course of running. In the world out there, we would be *evaluated* not only for the knowledge we would acquire, but also for how we presented our "selves." I would argue that her classroom was a site where students would be challenged, tested, called upon to achieve, and at times unfold....

You see, to navigate in the competitive world, students ought to learn certain meanings and codes—but, most importantly, I argue that they ought to unfold. Of course, in this world, learning the codes and certain meanings constitute part of our becoming—of our achieving. I strongly believe that that teacher cared deeply for and about us. She understood that in order to survive and thrive in this hierarchical world of agonistic becomings, we would need much more than academic knowledge. *Achieving* was a serious preoccupation in that educational milieu.

I struggled in the course of that year to just "pass" in that subject. I knew that a grade a little bit over 6.0 out of 10.0 would enable me to "make the cut." Back then, reaching anything beyond that pass mark was an ambitious goal—and not only in that subject. Students coming from various backgrounds—including the 'privileged' ones—would find themselves dwelling in the "in-between" of pass and failure—in the "in-between" created by the course of curriculum-as-plan. In subjects such as Portuguese, Chemistry, Physics, the course of schooling would be demanding on us. We were equally demanding of ourselves, too.

In one of my first English exams, I had already learned many English words, but I was unable to make sense of texts. I received it back with red-ink letters: "study more." Fortunately, the teacher did not write those words and let me hang in limbos of failure and destitution. She actively participated in tutoring activities and also carried out weekly volunteer classes where she would teach students English and codes through music (initially afraid of those encounters, I started to crave for them towards the end of year). Over time, she would help me perceive evaluations as an opportunity to achieve (more). Slowly, I was able to change my mindset in regards to evaluations. Evaluations were not only intrinsically connected to failure then, but to achieving. The object *could* signify something "positive."

Indeed, in different classes, the object of examination would be attributed different meanings—meanings that would change throughout the course of time. In Portuguese, while receiving a grade above 6.0 in the first semester, I felt proud for being placed in a position of "as-equals" with some "over-achievers." That object, the evaluation, fluctuated my ego because I was placing my "self" in a ruler to *compare* my achievement with that of my peers. In English, the meanings that constituted the object fluctuated more often because I did not always "excel." When I had finally learned "the basics," I saw my own progress and became proud of my "self" for having overcome hurdles to become "fluent": achievement (grades) became an object of its own, produced by another object (the exam), being ultimately placed *in relation* to the "self." Yet, at some point, I began to attribute "positive" meanings not *in relation to* the "self," but *in comparison to* "others." In other words, the exam and the meanings that it conveyed became not a nexus for relationality (with self), but the means for comparability (with alterity).

The meanings attributed to grades and exams changed according to the class—how the teacher positioned/perceived the exam; how we perceived the teacher, the subject, and, consequently, the examination; how much we have prepared for the examination; which grade we received in the exam, etc.— and those who would collectively make "the curve." Later, in college, having already learned well the importance of grades, I would pay clos(er) attention to that "object" to achieve (more). Even though I had become more *consciente* during those years, my relationship and the meanings that I attributed to that object had already been fixed: not only I aspired to achieve to be able to provide for better life conditions to my family, but I also wanted to show to "others" that if *I* could achieve, so could they. I wanted to demonstrate that achievement was a possibility, a reality that everyone could gauge—in a way, I wanted people to believe in the democratic tenet of upward mobility, and in meritocracy, too.

In Japan, my relationship with the "object" would become a little bit more contentious. I would dwell in a world of "in-betweens" in my daily

Japanese language classes: They were difficult and yet pleasant. As a *gakusei*, I had to study *hiragana*, *katakana*, and *kanji* every day before daily classes. The *sensei* would give his/her students drills to evaluate listening, writing, and grammar skills on a daily basis. Those drills would constitute part of our grades in the end of the semester. That approach to teaching required great attention and determination on our part. I also began to study new subjects such as microeconomics. Without prior knowledge, the teacher would employ basic calculus to explain the behaviour of the small firm. *Derivative? What the heck was that?*

Realizing that some students were "better off" in terms of mobilizing academic knowledge in the field of mathematics to make sense of "reality," I felt betrayed by my own educational system and, thus, I employed my judgemental thinking to blame it for the hurdles I experienced—*How come I did not study that stuff in high school like the other students from other countries?* I was placing the entire responsibility for "not knowing" on the system because, in a way, students are often stripped from the opportunity to run the course of complicated conversations in classrooms. In fact, they are often inclined to learn *exactly* what is mandated/validated in the curriculum/textbooks and evaluated in the exams. Unfortunately, in the world of schooling, the curriculum-as-plan can eclipse imagination, creativity, and the desire to "seek con(texts)" to "see the world big" (Greene, 1995)—the forging of an autobiographical lexis focused on relationality and contextuality.

In Japan, the object of "evaluation" would not only distribute fixed meanings as it occurred in other con(texts); exams would also demonstrate that I had severed my relationship with certain types of academic knowledge (e.g. number theory) in the course of running. Perhaps the examination produced some sort of "deficit-thinking" (Valencia, 1997), but, above all, it also demonstrated that I needed to run several other miles if I aspire to unfold my "self" in certain directions. Returning to the United States after my exchange experience, I decided to enroll in a calculus course and revisit my relationship with the field of mathematics (which was pretty wanting). I desired to understand how I could employ it to make a little bit more of sense of the "world," of "self," and "alterity." At that point, I believe that I was employing a type of "self-evaluation" to unfold my own course of running.

As a curricularist, I now understand that "achieving" is connected not only with lived experiences of becoming (curriculum as lived), but also with "curriculum development" (curriculum-as-plan) and with theories of change associated with standardization and teacher policies (see, for example, Mourshed et al., 2010). For example, standardization initiatives in the United States and in Brazil have alluded to a theory wherein the crafting of curriculum-as-plan should secure a minimum learning threshold to be achieved by all learners in each discipline. In other words, some level of standardization is perceived as a "right" because it allows students from across all spectrums of diversity *to achieve* at least *the minimum* level of learning deemed necessary for participation in a (competitive) polity (Jales Coutinho, 2021). That way, students, especially the most vulnerable, are not put in greater *comparative disadvantage* with their counterparts.

Based on qualitative data, Valencia (2020) underscored the fact that Brazilian students who had studied at a private school—and who therefore were positioned in more privileged con(texts)—experienced a different kind of schooling than their public counterparts. Private school students had been exposed to oral and other forms of self-expression, experimentation, and investigation, rather than just route work and memorization. Conversely, students in counterpart public schools from working-class families experienced a "different pattern of pedagogy and control" (Valencia, 2020, p. 95): they spent their time doing solitary seatwork, answering working sheets, and answering teachers' commands. Valencia (2020) also put in check the widespread perception that students from low socioeconomic households are intellectually inferior, and this "discrimination is likely more potent in mathematics compared to other school subjects of the curriculum" (p. 98).

If students are exposed to different curricula and to more academic knowledge and auspicious experiences than others, one can argue that schools are not truly advancing democracy. On the other hand, if students are exposed to the same curriculum-as-plan, one can argue that schools are not paying attention to con(texts) and cherishing diversity. Policymakers usually fluctuate in this contentious terrain of "in-betweens." Of course, students from a higher economic background can still look for opportunities to achieve *beyond* the threshold predetermined by standardization. "Shadow education" (Kim & Jung, 2022) demonstrates that parents (and students) are willing to do just that: they often try to achieve (more), not (less). People attempt to achieve more in comparison to those who make the curve. In a way, standardization is implemented to advance the promise of equality and opportunity in a democracy. Whether standardization is able to advance and deliver such promise is an open question, however.

As a curricularist, I understand the importance of offering students and educators trails for the unfolding; the importance of pointing out where the running can take place—especially for students who might not have been exposed to academic knowledge at home. Of course, we never know where a trail might take a student, for s/he can continuously unfold her/his autobiographical lexis to uncover new, not-yet-traveled pathways. In fact, this should be the aspiration of our Post-Reconceptualist enterprise: that students run their course and share with the collective what they experienced during their study, their unfolding, disseminating questions and supporting their peers in the course of running. The curriculum-as-plan should therefore be crafted to *distribute* academic knowledge—in specialized academic disciplines if you wish—while providing time and space for autobiographical unfolding: regressive, progressive, analytical, and synthetical moments, bifocalized altogether for new becomings, from a fortified nexus of love.

While the curriculum-as-plan may provide some levels of "orientation"—a compass for the mobilization of knowledge—the student will run her/his own course as s/he unfolds her autobiographical lexis: the unfolding of an autobiography *cannot* be standardized. The meanings that students attribute to their lives, the way through which they mobilize academic knowledge to unfold, which con(texts) they employ to bifocalize—*that* will be unique to each individual, to her/his moment in the trajectory, to her/his ancestors… The meanings that people attribute to the unfolding can certainly intersect, but the unfolding will differ in several other forms, such as style, tone, form (e.g. performative, writing), etc. *Would this constitute an adventure?* I believe so, but an adventure tantamount to unfolding and learning, not a disastrous one. I remember that, once exposed to the autobiographical con(text) in Phillips Exeter Academy through a course on creative writing, and mobilizing knowledge in the Harkness table, I was able to see my "self" a little bit more like a *seeker*, rather than a mere knower or doer. I argue that when students, educators, and decision-makers are committed to mobilizing knowledge and employing the autobiographical con(text) to "study" and "bifocalize," real change can occur in educational settings.

Here, I attempt to forge and to advance a collective project within Post-Reconceptualization which I have qualified as "autobiographying disciplinarity": a project that aims to turn the academic disciplines into malleable sites for "study" (Pinar, 2011), "bifocalization" (Jales Coutinho, 2022), and "unfolding" (Jales Coutinho, 2021): be it in the subjects of arts, chemistry, geography, history, languages, mathematics, physics, etc. In regards to actualization, I return to the meanings attribute to the object of "evaluation." As I have pointed out in the previous subsection, in the world of schooling, several evaluations are employed throughout the course in order to examine whether students are making "satisfactory" progress. The evaluations convey both internal *and* external meanings in the educational system. Actualization, on the other hand, describes the capacity of the individual *to realize* his/her own unfolding in the course of running *in relation to* "self," "others," "nature" and "the cosmos." Indeed, actualization constitutes the moment(s) in which the individual "studies" and "bifocalizes," becoming:

(i) *Consciente* of her/his autobiographical unfolding, of the circuits of privilege and oppression that constitute the course,
(ii) Aware of his/her capabilities and knowledge, and, based on this understanding,
(iii) Mindful of the need to seek novel con(texts) in form of knowledge *and* experiences to continue running and dwelling, unfolding his/her autobiographical journey—this *cosmopolitan* character of curriculum—to (re)construct the subject.

At this point, I highlight points (ii) and (iii) because they are strictly connected to curriculum-as-plan (and standardization). I argue that curriculum-as-plan should *indicate* which types of knowledge and which trails students and educators might take in their own unfolding—which, at the end of the day, will be non-standardized. Again, the curriculum-as-plan may be particular helpful for those who might not have access to a myriad of academic knowledge at home, where opportunities and experiences may be circumscribed by budget constraints, just as an example. Educators may support students writing and engaging with academic knowledge as they dwell with concepts in the disciplines to unfold their autobiographical lexis—be it via creative writing, singing, dancing, etc.

For example, I have recently discussed the meaning of "patterns" with a student. The student was fascinated with mathematics and wanted to mobilize academic knowledge to describe how she perceived and engaged with this concept/subject to understand her world and unfolding. In her short autobiographical account, she searched for meanings in regressive, progressive, analytical and synthetical moments. She (re)constructed her "self" also finding meanings for her work as a prospective college student. We talked about her educational and life experiences; we discussed where she found patters/sequences in her life; we talked about the sequences that she was able to visualize in her trajectory to school, and which events/objects constituted such patterns.

During our conversations, we also discussed the significance of patterns in mathematics (e.g. whether we could identify a patter in an exponential function like in a sine function—the moment at which I pointed out that the exponential function was "increasing at an increasing rate"), and the meaning of "randomness." She underscored the appreciation for the Fibonacci sequence. Then, we talked about the role of statistics in identifying patterns in natural/social phenomena (e.g. the frequency of hurricane landfall in North America, and the possible creation of technological systems for pre-emptive warnings), as well as the construction of statistical models. Finally, we discussed where and how she could seek con(texts) (in the form of academic knowledge) to further her own understanding of "self" and "patterns," and how she could mobilize this knowledge for new becomings—personal and collective. These were ongoing conversations, moments in which I also unfolded my own relational understanding/ relationship with mathematics and sciences.

One may argue that "actualization" is tantamount to "lifelong learning" discourses. However, actualization goes *beyond* discourses on lifelong learning due to several reasons. For example, in CWSJL, I argued that autobiography is the heart of education. Actualization departs from such a premise; it positions autobiographical unfolding as paramount to self- and collective-awakening. Lifelong learning discourses may encompass callings for individuals to brush up on their "skills" to serve a project that might not necessarily be aligned with Post-Reconceptualization as a collective public moral enterprise (e.g. a project that does not espouse love and reconciliation). Indeed, actualization also encompasses critical agencies, from a fortified nexus of love. Hence, I propose an additional layer to it. To "actualize" signifies the moments in which the individual, from his/her critical agency, and departing from a nexus of love, becomes:

(iv) Willing to embrace and exude caregiving as relational and contextual means for personal and collective unfolding and awakening—a proposition which may support our path towards reconciliation (with self, alterity, nature, the sacred/spiritual, and the cosmos) in the course *of* development.

Actualization should therefore signify more "internal" meanings (meaning to the individual who runs his/her course in solitude and with others) than "external" ones (meaning to an external body that needs to "evaluate" whether the individual has reached a specific mark in a specific course).

When someone becomes "actualized," s/he understands that the unfolding is never complete: quoting Maxine Greene, "I am who I am not *yet*" (Maxine Greene, in Pinar, 2008, p. 151). Concomitantly, s/he becomes *sensitive* and *reflexive* to/about *each* relational encounter in the course. One becomes critically aware of one's "giving" to the land and to those who are a part of it, including the "self." In a world of actualization, love become less like a negotiation and more like a symbiotic act of (just) giving. In this historical moment, the collective would understand, appreciate, and cherish the ethical relationality of giving care for *collective* thriving, unfolding, and sustenance. There would be no difference between personal and collective: everything would constitute a fluid channel of (just) giving. Moreover, because people would become aware of their unfolding and of their capabilities and knowledge from the outset (always limited and incomplete), people would continue to seek con(texts) as part of their natural state of *being* in the world. External evaluations would become obsolete in this historical moment because the individual would guide his/her own unfolding, his/her seeking, departing to new con(texts), in solitude and with others, in formal and informal settings.

Although external evaluations could be initially employed to point out "knowledge deviances," the individual would become more interested in finding out and working through these "deviances" in collective conversations and in ludic activities with educators and peers, and later in his/her own study. Of course, in this scenario, the teaching profession would need to be perceived not only as a "caregiving" profession, but as an intellectual one—as it rightly should. Eventually, once the majority of the population attained greater levels of *conscientização* and actualized, external evaluations—which are employed to convey meanings to stakeholders usually placed *outside* the school (even though teachers are encouraged to use assessments to evaluate their "performance" and to employ teaching "strategies" that can best serve their students in the *achievement* of educational goals/marks, it is the policymaker who is often interested in external evaluations, for these can support the design of several policies including merit pay)—would become less valuable to societies.

People everywhere would understand the significance of knowledge mobilization in autobiography via study and bifocalization. Hence, the citizenry would mobilize knowledge with others to unfold continuously in the world—with their offspring, family members, friends, colleagues, etc. Parents would read to their children, converse with them, speak about their ancestors, about forms of knowledge creation, etc. Such conversations would constitute our situatedness of becoming in "private" and "public" spheres from the outset. People would trust/be confident that students and educators—who would then perceive and build the profession as a "caregiving" and "intellectual" enterprise—would collectively unfold in formal educational settings, too. The external meanings of evaluations would be gradually replaced by actualization. This may look like a puzzling image to policymakers and the citizenry in the world of today, but here I theorize about a progressive world where (i) people would have already engaged in study and bifocalization (see CWSJL), attaining greater levels of *conscientização*, and a place where (ii) trust and love would be proliferated rather than negotiated.

Indeed, we live quite in a different world from the one described above. In our antagonistic, agonistic, and competitive world of becomings—one which produces a lot of daily interactions and where "presentism" (Pinar, 2019, p. 32) constitutes one of our habits of being and becoming—one may argue that actualization is yet to constitute our mode of being and becoming in the world. Moreover, because some people have little access to multifaceted knowledge via the curriculum-as-plan and through their interactions at home and in the community—here, the canonical curriculum question reverberates: "*which knowledge is of most worth?*" (Pinar, 2019, p. 31)—, this world would become possible under some conditions. For example, schools and societies would need to initiate a collective, public project where individuals from all strata would be able to access and mobilize knowledge via the curriculum-as-plan (see, for example, Wheelahan, 2015). Moreover, this would require a significant shift in how knowledge is treated under neoliberal regimes: knowledge would need to be perceived as part of our educational commons rather than a special commodity for the privileged few—people in the community and across all spectrums of diversity would be able to access and mobilize knowledge *with* the support of educational settings across the lifespan. Places such as libraries would become revitalized settings for collective unfolding in knowledge societies, and people would treat these as indispensible sites for collective thriving, for the upholding of human dignity.

Because our world looks so different, we ought to engage decision-makers in this complicated conversation to position curriculum as a collective public moral enterprise in our schools. Moreover, we can *aspire* to become a better version of our own relational selves in the course of running, and *inspire* one "self" and others to join this course—from a fortified nexus of love, running towards love and justice—so that can we collectively think *and* actualize "development" otherwise. As curricularists, I contend that we ought to be attentive to transitions and to single thoughts. When we engage in "autobiographying disciplinarity," we may, in a way, engage in a process of "de-standardization," giving students more opportunities to mobilize knowledge to unfold their relational and contextual autobiographies, engage in complicated conversations, and (re)construct the subject— working from within while looking outwards. However, these same students might still experience some level/form of curriculum standardization because educators and students may not yet have acquired/ experienced the phenomena of knowledge mobilization to forge relational and contextual autobiographies in educational settings (and beyond). Study and bifocalization require an ongoing commitment to self and alterity because curriculum as a collective public moral enterprise constitutes an ongoing project.

References

Bar-Tal, D. (2000). From intractable conflict through Conflict Resolution to reconciliation: Psychological analysis. *Political Psychology, 21*(2), 351–365. https://doi.org/10.1111/0162-895x.00192

Brown, C., & Ainley, K. (2009). *Understanding international relations* (4th ed.). Palgrave.

Burns, J. P. (2018). *Power, curriculum, and embodiment: Re-thinking curriculum as counter-conduct and counter-politics.* Palgrave Macmillan.

Clarke, M. (2012). *What matters most for student assessment systems: A framework paper.* The World Bank.

Côté, R., Denis, J., Watts, V., & Wilkes, R. (2021). Indigenization, institutions, and imperatives: Perspectives on reconciliation from the CSA decolonization sub-committee. *Canadian Review of Sociology/Revue Canadienne De Sociologie, 58*(1), 105–117. https://doi.org/10.1111/cars.12325

Davidson, P. M. (2018). *Secondary social studies curriculum in post-genocide Rwanda as mediated by Unesco and Post-Holocaust education in Germany* (dissertation). ProQuest Dissertations & Theses, Ann Arbor.

Freedman, M. H., Langbein, J. H., & Cohen, E. D. (2010). The adversary system and the practice of law. In J. Arthur & W. H. Shaw (Eds.), *Readings in the philosophy of law* (5th ed., pp. 1–21). Pearson.

Fuller, L. (2010). Eight ways to fail to make law. In J. Arthur & W. H. Shaw (Eds.), *Readings in the philosophy of law* (5th ed., pp. 27–31). Essay, Pearson.

Golding, W. (2018). Lord of the flies: A moral allegory. In L. P. Pojman & L. Vaughn (Eds.), *The moral life: An introductory reader in ethics and literature* (6th ed., pp. 10–30). Oxford University Press.

Green, T. F. (1980). *Predicting the behavior of the educational system.* Syracuse University Press.

Greene, M. (1995). *Releasing the imagination: Essays on education, the arts, and social change.* Jossey-Bass Publishers.

Hambleton, R. K., & Jones, R. W. (1993). Comparison of classical test theory and item response theory and their applications to test development. *Educational Measurement: Issues and Practice, 12*(3), 38–47. https://doi.org/10.1111/j.1745-3992.1993.tb00543.x

Jales Coutinho, A. M. (2021). The missing context for justice in social science education: 'Autobiographying' disciplinarity in a post-pandemic world. In A. Samuels, & G. L. Samuels (Eds.), Fostering diversity and inclusion in the social sciences (pp. 237–250). IAP Publishing.

Jales Coutinho, A. M. (2022). *Curriculum work and social justice leadership in a post-reconceptualist era: Attaining critical consciousness and learning to become* (1st ed.). Routledge. https://doi.org/10.4324/9781003188629

Joireman, S. F. (2004). Colonization and the rule of law: Comparing the effectiveness of common law and civil law countries. *Constitutional Political Economy, 15*(4), 315–338. https://doi.org/10.1007/s10602-004-7766-7

Jung, J.-H. (2016). *The concept of care in curriculum studies: Juxtaposing Currere and Hakbeolism*. Routledge.

Kim, Y. C., & Jung, J.-H. (2022). *Theorizing shadow education and academic success in East Asia: Understanding the meaning, value, and use of shadow education by East Asian students*. Routledge.

Laeuchli, U. M. (2007). Civil and common law: Contrast and synthesis in international arbitration. *Dispute Resolution Journal, 62*(3), 81–85. Retrieved fromhttps://www.proquest.com/scholarly-journals/civil-common-law-contrast-synthesis-international/docview/198101491/se-2?accountid=41734

Luckesi, C. C. (2011). *Avaliação da aprendizagem: componente do ato pedagógico* (1st ed.). Cortez Editora.

Merryman, J., & Pérez-Perdomo, R. (2007). *The civil law tradition: An introduction to the legal systems of Europe and Latin America* (3rd ed.). Stanford University Press.

Morigiwa, Y. (2015). Making delivery a priority: A philosophical perspective on corruption and strategy for remeda. In J. Wouters, A. Ninio, H. Cissé, & T. Doherty (Eds.), *Improving delivery in development: The role of voice, social contract, and accountability* (Vol. 6, pp. 437–456). World Bank Group.

Morigiwa, Y., Stolleis, M., & Halpérin, J.-L. (Eds.). (2013). *Interpretation of law in the age of enlightenment: From the rule of the king to the rule of law*. Springer.

Mourshed, M., Chijioke, C., & Barber, M. (2010). *How the world's most improved school systems keep getting better*. McKinsey & Company.

OECD. (2013). *Oecd reviews of evaluation and assessment in education-synergies for better learning: An international perspective on evaluation and assessment*. OECD Publishing.

Pinar, W. (Ed.). (2010). *Curriculum studies in South Africa: Intellectual histories & present circumstances*. Palgrave Macmillan.

Pinar, W. F. (2008). *Intellectual advancement through disciplinarity: Verticality and horizontality in curriculum*. Sense Publishers.

Pinar, W. F. (2011). The *character of curriculum studies: Bildung, currere, and the recurring question of the subject*. Palgrave Macmillan.

Pinar, W. F. (2019). *What is curriculum theory?*. Routledge.

Posel, D. (2001). Article What's in a name? Racial categorisations under apartheid and their afterlife. *Transformation: Critical Perspectives on Southern Africa, 47*, 50–74. https://digital.lib.msu.edu/projects/africanjournals/html/itemdetail.cfm?recordID=785

Rocha, S. D. (2020). *The syllabus as curriculum: A reconceptualist approach* (1st ed.). Routledge. https://doi.org/10.4324/9780429027901

Roth, A. (2017). Machine testimony. *The Yale Law Journal, 126*(7), 1972–2053. https://www.yalelawjournal.org/article/machine-testimony

Schneider, J., & Hutt, E. (2013). Making the grade: A history of the A–F marking scheme. *Journal of Curriculum Studies, 46*(2), 201–224. https://doi.org/10.1080/00220272.2013.790480

Soudien, C. (2010). "What to teach the natives": A historiography of the curriculum dilemma in South Africa. In W. Pinar (Ed.), *Curriculum studies in south africa: Intelectual histories and present circumstances* (pp. 19–46). Palgrave Macmillan.

Sousa, L. A., & Braga, A. E. (2020). Teoria clássica dos testes e teoria de resposta ao item EM Avaliação Educacional. *Revista De Instrumentos, Modelos e Políticas Em Avaliação Educacional, 1*(1). https://doi.org/10.51281/impa.e020002

Stein, S., Andreotti, V., Ahenakew, C., & Hunt, D. (2022). The complexities and paradoxes of decolonization in Education. *Reimagining Globalization and Education*, 198–213. https://doi.org/10.4324/9781003207528-14

Taft, L. (2000). Apology subverted: The commodification of apology. *The Yale Law Journal, 109*(5), 1135. https://doi.org/10.2307/797485

United Nations. (1994). *Security council RESOLUTION 955 (1994)*. New York: United Nations Security Council. https://unictr.irmct.org/sites/unictr.org/files/legal-library/941108_res955_en.pdf

Vago, S. (2009). *Law and society* (9th ed.). Pearson.

Valencia, R. R. (1997). *The evolution of deficit thinking: Educational thought and practice*. Falmer Press.

Valencia, R. R. (2020). *International deficit thinking: Educational thought and practice*. Routledge.

Wheelahan, L. (2015). Not just skills: What a focus on knowledge means for vocational education. *Journal of Curriculum Studies, 47*(6), 750–762. https://doi.org/10.1080/00220272.2015.1089942

Wolff, P., & Braman, O. (1999). Traditional dispute resolution in Micronesia. *South Pacific Journal of Psychology, 11*(1), 44–53. https://doi.org/10.1017/S0257543400000742

World Bank Group. (2018). *World development report 2018: Learning to realize education's promise*. International Bank for Reconstruction and Development/The World Bank.

Zorbas, E. (2004). Reconciliation in post-genocide Rwanda. *African Journal of Legal Studies, 1*(1), 29–52. https://doi.org/10.1163/221097312x13397499735904

6 Conclusion: Love and reconciliation

To fortify a nexus of love to run the course: *Are we better off by becoming takers rather than givers? How will I ever be able to work alongside alterity when people seem to deliberately corrode trust to look after their own welfare? How can I know that my "self" can love when that same "self" self-questions care?* To give love in this course *of* development is certainly a labor of courage.

Indeed, to care for and about those who might have hurt "self" and beloved "others" demands a lot of work from *within*, a (re)construction of "self" and of all sentiments that are able to bind, including trust. I can think of many instances where this situation may seem impossible. But again, *How are we going to predict the unfolding? How are we going to determine where our relational encounters will lead us?* The best we can do is to work to fortify this nexus of love, to become more studious, humble, relational, contextual—and to trust that this labor (and disposition) will shape the course. In this unfolding, as we attempt to face that bridge feeling a little bit more anew, we also seek to reconcile with that very course, with "self," "alterity," "nature," and the "cosmos." Hopefully, certain types of reconciliation(s) may be able to change the course itself—for those who are yet to come, for those who are yet to run it.

At school and at home, students and teachers may struggle with hidden scars and meanings that nobody might be aware of—meanings that may diverge from "caregiving" and which may prevent the proliferation of love and the forging of reconciliation. For example, learning about gender and sexuality in a science class, students may be invited to watch a lesson about productive health. They might observe a health practitioner demonstrate how students can wear a condom to protect themselves from sexual transmitted diseases (STDs) and from unplanned pregnancy. While the demonstration may be designed to support health practices at the outset, such a demonstration could

DOI: 10.4324/9781003359968-6

elicit undesirable meanings and feelings in a small population of students who might have been abused in the past and, consequently, traumatized. Indeed, although the activity may constitute a curriculum policy (if we teach students how to wear condoms properly, they will more likely be able to protect themselves), the activity and the objects that constitute it can elicit disturbing feelings and memories in a vulnerable population. The very activity that is meant to protect may, in fact, set some students farther away from moments of learning and healing—from walking the path of reconciliation… reconciliation with the world which seemingly *chooses* to hurt rather than care.

The classroom is a site for complexity, a place where individuals are constantly learning and mobilizing knowledge, attributing (new) meanings to objects according to their subjectivementalities—converging and diverging ongoingly, and not always from a fortified nexus of love toward care. For the classroom to become a locus of love (and reconciliation) in this course of agonistic, antagonistic, and competitive becomings, educators must be attuned with their subjectivementalities and with the students they aspire to serve. Indeed, in any circumstance, a teacher devoted to social justice education must remain vigilant to con(texts) and "read" which kinds of meanings students attribute to activities and objects. In the activity to promote health habits, the teacher could ask: *Are some students joking and laughing about the activity? If so, why? Do some students seem uncomfortable or unwilling to participate in dialogues? Is it because of the jokes, or because of the activity per se? Could it be something that has been said and presented which might have released traumatic memories?*

If judgementality was employed in such a con(text)—e.g. "you are not participating like the other students because you are not an engaged one" and "you laughed at it because you are ignorant"— that small population of students would probably feel more disconnected with the classroom. Seeking con(texts) and becoming *consciente* of classroom interactions, of the meanings that constitute the texts that unfold in the classroom, is essential for this Post-Reconceptualization era of curriculum studies. Without a doubt, the teacher must be attentive to meanings and dedicate her/his time to build relational encounters with students so that trust and care permeate such relationships, from a fortified nexus of love. In an activity such as this, it would be important, for example, for the educator to share information on what resources were available, and what students could do/who they could reach out to at school and in the broader community in case someone had already engaged in a relationship where consent was not given and/or respected, etc.

It is also important to note that those who contribute to this Post-Reconceptualist conversation as a collective public moral enterprise are engaging their "selves" in "public service" (Pinar, 2010)—whether or not they are physically located in the public sector—to create a nexus for curriculum from a fortified nexus of love. Curricularists who uncover and face (at times painful) memories in their labor (e.g. writing, researching, teaching, designing policies, etc.) are engaging in an act of courage because they might have to (re)live/revisit relational encounters with undesired meanings to actualize a world otherwise. It should take the courage of a whole collective though, of an expansive constellation of care—in academia, in offices, in schools… places everywhere—to build this Post-Reconceptualist project of curriculum as a collective public moral enterprise.

As curricularists, we should be conscious of the *negotiations* we make in the course of running, of the way we go about loving in our relational encounters—with "self," "alterity," "nature," and the "cosmos". In a world of antagonistic, agonistic, and competitive becomings, we ought to find ways within the self to *proliferate* love *with* others. Running and dwelling, we put our hearts on the front line of our daily actions, in every step we take in the course and on that bridge, mobilizing "the what" (knowledge) so that "the way" (the course) becomes less like a locus for "judicious interpretation," and more like a nexus for relational and contextual encounters: a locus for/of love and reconciliation, a place for self and collective awakening, a nexus for new becomings.

Reference

Pinar, W. F. (2010). *The worldliness of a cosmopolitan education: Passionate lives in public service*. Routledge, Taylor & Francis Group.

Index

Pages in *italics* refer figures.

acquisitive society 25
actualization 7, 66, 82–85, 89, 96, 101–103, 105
adversary system 90, 95
altruism 21
analytical moment 55–56
ancient lexis 15
Anglo-American nexus 25
antagonism 94
anthropocene 41
anthropological work 40
Aoki, T. T. 5, 36, *37*, 38
autobiographical con(text) 6, 8, 13, 51, 84, 96, 101
autobiographical lexis 6–7, 42, 46, 50, 56, 75–76, 82, 99, 101–102
autobiographical understanding(s) 2, 13, 56, 82, 85
autobiographying discourses 49

beauty 19, 40
becoming 1–7, 18, 24, 28–29, 35–36, 40, 42, 44–45, 47–51, 55–62, 64–65, 67–69, 72–74, 76–79, 81–83, 88–89, 91, 92, 93, 95–97, 101–105, 109, 110–111
Berman, L. M. 20
Bible 56, 60–61, 63
bifocalizing 1–2, 6, 36–37, 50–51, 55, 63, 101–102, 104, 106
bifocal vision 68
BIPOC ethics of care 49
Bishop, Owis 42–43

Bitter Milk: Women and Teaching 58
Bobbitt, J. F. 15, 27
Brazilian policymaker 59

Canadian Society for the Study of Education (CSSE) 38
caregiving 3, 36, 47, 57, 63–66, 68, 82, 86, 103–104, 109
capability 5, 39–41
Catholic church 61
Catholicism 61; tenets of 60–61
Chatzidakis, A. 43
cisheteronormative assumptions 42
classical test theory (CTT) 87
collective public moral enterprise 1, 8, 14, 37, 51, 56–57, 62, 65, 75, 82, 85, 89, 93, 103, 105–106, 111
comparison 27, 48, 84, 94, 98, 100
conscientização crítica 21
constellation of responsibilities 26
constellations of care 42, 48, 59, 67
contract theory 86–87
convergence 5, 42, 47, 49–50, *50*, 57, 62–64, 67, 70, 76
conversation 17, 21; complicated 29, 49, 56; intra and intergenerational 38; skills of 17; vehicle for 18
cordial relations 26
course of development 1–2, 4, 6, 8, 11–13, 15, 19, 27–29, 34, 36, 39–42, 47, 49–50, 55–56, 64, 76–78, 82

Index 113

Covid-19 pandemic 88
crises 75–79
critical agency 82, 103
critical bifocality 6, 12, 28, 38, 41
criticality 3, 36
critical juncture 5, 13
critical thinking 34
cultural capital 11, 46
currere 5, 11–13, 25, 43, 45, 47, 56, 73
curriculum 4, 43; Aoki's contributions 38; -as-plan 14, 101, 105; concept 3; crisis of 76; "love" in 14–29; policies 83, 86, 110; Post-Reconceptualist era of 82; Reconceptualization era of 66; as shadow 45; studies 6; subjects 66; understanding of 13
curriculum-as-lived 14
curriculum-as-plan 14, 82, 85, 93, 97, 99–102, 105
Curriculum Studies Handbook: The Next Moment 11, 25
CWSJL 1–2, 5–6, 27, 34, 39, 49, 67, 72, 75–77, 85, 87

Dalai Lama's theory 25
decision-making 46, 49, 68
decolonial indigenization 91
difference 1, 5, 8, 12–14, 23–24, 39, 40–41, 49, 59, 62, 66, 76, 87, 90–91, 104
disciplinary tactics 88
divergence 5, 46, *50*, 59, 62–63, 77–78
Du Bois, W. E. B. 28
dwell 2–3, 13, 27, 36, 38–39, 42, 48, 51, 57, 63, 65, 73–76, 78, 82, 83, 85, 97, 102, 111
Dyer, P. 20

Edgerton, S. H. 23–24
education: caregivers 83; gaps 66; multicultural approaches to 23; nature of 93; public approach to 47; religious 62; settings 51; shadow 45, 100
ethical-based love commitment 25
ethical self-encounters 12
ethics of care 1, 3–6, 12, 27, 34–51, 56, 94
eugenicist ideas 15

European Credit Transfer and Accumulation System (ECTS) 95
evaluations 7-8, 46, 81–87, 97–106; in the world of legal systems 89–94; in the world of school systems 94–96
examination 45–46, 88, 98–99

feminist lens 23
Field, J. C. 8
Flowers, R. 26
fortification 1, 3–6, 8, 27, 56, 78; of love 1, 6, 8, 35
Freire, Paulo 21
Frymier, J. R. 20
Fuller, L. 86

Gallagher, Kathleen 2
Galloway, C. M. 19
Gaztambide-Fernández, R. A. 2
generalization, lessons in 86–87
gig economy 73
governmentality: Foucauldian concept of 84; legality and 92; objects of 89; tool of 95
greater standardization 95
Grumet, M. R. 58

Hakbeolism 11, 43
Hakbeolismo 43
Hakim, J. 43
Halperin, D. M. 76
Hattam, R. 25
hierarchization 3
hierarchy 5, 39
historical debts 66
hooks, b. 14, 23–24, 26, 28
horizontal structures 3, 13
hospitality 2, 4, 27–28, 35, 41, 48, 76–78
Howard, Ron 68
Huebner, D. E. 16–18, 22, 27

in-betweenness 36–37, 49, 51, 56, 58, 71
indigenous scholarship 25–26
internationalization 4–5, 38

In *The Lure of the Transcendent: Collected Essays by Dwayne E. Huebner* 16
Irwin, R. L. 36
item response theory (IRT) 87

judgementalities 2, 7, 89, 93–94
judgementality 66, 84, 89, 92, 110
Jung, Carl 19
Jung, J.-H. 5, 11, 43, 45, 47, 82
juxtaposition 3–4, 11–29, 73–74, 84

Kamani, F. 76
Keith, N. 26
key technology of educational bureaucratization 94
Kim, Y. C. 45
kindness 16, 21
Kramp, D. 21

labor of love 5, 7–8, 74, 79
Lack, C. A. 19
land 40-41, 57, 104
language of opposition 24
law 1, 7, 27, 63, 65–66, 78, 81–83, 85-87, 89–90, 92
Lee, N. Y. S. 38
lexis 2, 25–28, 42, 56, 78
(neo)liberalism 3
lifelong discourses 16
Lingering with the Works of Ted T. Aoki: Historical and Contemporary Significance for Curriculum Research and Practice 38
Littler, J. 43
love 22, 24–27; as an analogy for teaching and learning 24; as an ethics of care/giving 34–51; both in regression and progression 40; brotherhood 66–68; conceptualization of 21, 23; crisis of 76; deliberations on 23; essence of 18; fortification of 78–79; as genesis 3, 5, 28, 34, 42, 56; Hooks' deliberations on 25; and justice 81–106; kindness 16; for knowledge 15; labor 72–75; of learning 16; parental 57–60; and reconciliation 22–23, 109–111; religious 60–66; returning to 56; romantic 69–72; teaching children to 20–21; understanding of 18–19
Love and compassion: Exploring their role in education 15
Love in the Post-Reconceptualist Era of Curriculum Work: Deliberations on the Meanings of Care 8
Luckesi, C. C. 89

machismos 58
Malewski, E. 11
Marable, M. 28
Mason, Charlotte 15
Merryman, J. 92
Miller, Jack 2
Miller, J. E. 11
Miller, J. P. 15
mobilization of knowledge/knowledge mobilization 94, 66, 101, 104, 106
mode of inquiry 12
movement of convergence 50

nation-state 5, 27, 77, 89–90
negotiation 5, 41–42, 56, 104, 111
nexus 13; forge and fortify 51; of love 13, 36, 39, 47; sanguine vision of 36
Nitobe Memorial Garden (NMG) 36–37
Noddings, N. 43–45

Oliveira, G. 42
ongoing ethical engagement with alterity 36
openness and receptivity 22
Owis, B. 43

Patriotism 15
Pedagogia do Oprimido 21
Pérez-Perdomo, R. 92
performative autobiographical lexis 6
Piepzna-Samarasinha, L. L. 43
Pilder, W. F. 19

Pinar, W. F. 5, 11, 13–14, 16, 23, 47, 73
Popkewitz, T. S. 2, 39
positive, creative, and responsive strategies 20
post-reconceptualist 4; conversation 111; crises of curriculum 77; enterprise 101; era 49, 74; era in schools 96; project 46; project of curriculum 111; tenets 14, 25, 38; theories 83
post-reconceptualization 1, 5, 35, 46, 65; actualization in 85, 89, 96–106; era of curriculum studies 110
power sharing 78
power shifting 78
praxis 2
primitive tribes 15
proliferation 5, 8, 56, 75–79, 86, 109
public moral enterprise 7

quality of disposability 44
queer ethics of care 43
queer 7, 42–43, 49, 69, 71–72, 76
Queer, Trans, Black, Indigenous, People of Color (QTBIPOC) 42
Quinn, Molly 2
Quran 64

real site of education 5–6, 12–13
reconceptualist movement 14
reconciliation 1–2, 4, 7–8, 22–23, 27, 83, 91, 93, 103, 109–111
religious hermeneutics of love 65
religious hermeneutics of violence 65
Reynolds, W. M. 23
Rocha, S. D. 72, 88
Rottenberg, C. 43
run 2, 13, 27, 36, 38, 42, 57; the course 5–6, 8, 45, 60, 63, 65, 77, 99, 109

Schubert, W. H. 2, 23, 25
sedimentation 38
Segal, L. 43
self-actualization 82
self-aggrandizing absorptivity 36
self-evaluations 7, 82, 94, 96
servant-served paradigm 2
sexual transmitted diseases (STDs) 109

skepticism 36
Slattery, P. 23
Smith, Liesa Griffin 2
Snaza, N. 2, 25
social cohesion 82
social justice education 110
social justice lexicon 81
Strong-Wilson, T. 12
subjectivementalities 8, 42, 96, 110
subject reconstruction 22, 28
symbiotic constellations 42

Taubman, P. M. 23
Teaching the Young to Love 20
tenets of Catholicism 60–61
The Curriculum 15, 27
the good citizen 15
the ideal 35
Theory into Practice 19
Truth and Reconciliation Commission of Canada (TRC) 1
Truth and Reconciliation Commissions (TRCs) 91

Understanding curriculum: An introduction to the study of historical and contemporary curriculum discourses 23
understanding 43, 102; autobiographical 13; curriculum 4, 12–14, 23; in post-reconceptualization 3; of love 4–5, 14–29
United Nations Security Council 93
universal responsibility 26
University of British Columbia (UBC) 36, 75
University of Toronto 62
unplanned pregnancy 109
Ursino, J. M. 38

Vago, S. 82
Valencia, R. R. 100
vertical structures 3, 5, 12–14

Wallenberg, Raoul Gustaf 48
Whiteness 40–41, 55
Wong, L. E. 38

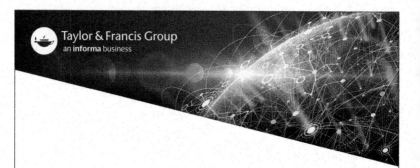